TRACING YOUR GEORGIAN ANCESTORS 1714–1837

TRACING YOUR GEORGIAN ANCESTORS 1714–1837

A Guide for Family Historians

John Wintrip

Pen & Sword
FAMILY HISTORY

First published in Great Britain in 2018 by
PEN & SWORD FAMILY HISTORY
an imprint of
Pen & Sword Books Ltd
47 Church Street
Barnsley
South Yorkshire
S70 2AS

ISBN 978 1 52670 422 1

A CIP catalogue record for this book is
available from the British Library

Typeset in (details of size & name of typeface) by (details of typesetter)

Printed and bound in (country) by (printer's details)

Pen & Sword Books Ltd incorporates the imprints of Pen & Sword
Archaeology, Atlas, Aviation, Battleground, Discovery, Family History,
History, Maritime, Military, Naval, Politics, Railways, Select, Social History,
Transport, True Crime, and Claymore Press, Frontline Books, Leo Cooper,
Praetorian Press, Remember When, Seaforth Publishing and Wharncliffe.

For a complete list of Pen & Sword titles please contact
PEN & SWORD BOOKS LIMITED
47 Church Street, Barnsley, South Yorkshire, S70 2AS, England
E-mail: enquiries@pen-and-sword.co.uk
Website: www.pen-and-sword.co.uk

CONTENTS

ACKNOWLEDGEMENTS

I would like to express my thanks to all my previous clients, who collectively have given me the opportunity to examine a far wider range of sources while researching their ancestors than would have been possible through personal research alone. I am also grateful to the staff of the large number of archives throughout the country where I have carried out both personal and professional research over many years. I would particularly like to register my gratitude to Jacky Casson, Karen Cummings, Judy Lester and Malcolm McEachran for reading through drafts of the text and making valuable suggestions. Finally, I would like to thank my wife Jessica for her constant support and encouragement while I was writing this book.

ABBREVIATIONS

The following abbreviations have been used throughout this book:

GRO   General Register Office
LDS   Church of Jesus Christ of Latter-day Saints (Mormons)
TNA   The National Archives

INTRODUCTION

Over two decades ago, as a relatively inexperienced researcher, I searched in vain for a book that focused specifically on research in the period immediately before civil registration. In the continuing absence of such a book, and after several years as a professional genealogist, I began to think about writing one myself. I subsequently came to the conclusion that two complementary but self-contained books might be more appropriate: one would describe the sources, and the other, aimed at more experienced researchers, would concentrate on research methods. As so little had been written on research methods, I decided to write that book first. *Tracing Your Pre-Victorian Ancestors: A Guide to Research Methods for Family Historians* was published by Pen & Sword in February 2017. I then turned my attention to the present book.

The aim of this book is to describe the sources available for researching ancestors in Georgian England. The period defined as the Georgian era is often considered to include the short reign of William IV, who died only a few days before civil registration was introduced in 1837. This definition is particularly apt in the context of family history research, and has therefore been used in the context of this book.

The genealogical sources surviving from the Georgian era are essentially the same as they were many decades ago, but what has changed, and has been increasing rapidly in recent years, is the availability of online search tools and digital images of sources. Online resources can enable research to be accomplished in hours that would previously have taken months or years, but the material available online represents only the tip of the iceberg, the size of which is dependent on the area of the country in which research is being carried out and specific characteristics of the individuals and families being investigated. Overcoming brick walls before 1837 often requires using sources that are only available in archives. Researchers are more likely to be able to find information about their ancestors by first identifying appropriate sources and then establishing how they can access them, rather than the other way around. Focusing only on sources available online, or only on those held in a conveniently located local archive, can result in significant information not being found.

As well as a fundamental change in sources, the transition from the Victorian to the Georgian era also involves a significant change in the relationship between genealogical research and historical background knowledge. The wider range of sources available after 1837 can enable researchers to identify their Victorian ancestors even with little or no knowledge of the historical background. In contrast, successful research before 1837 is often dependent on the possession of sufficient historical knowledge to enable the often meagre information in records to be understood, and to ensure that important clues are not overlooked. The core of essential knowledge consists of an eclectic combination of topics, rarely covered in any depth in mainstream history courses. This information has been gathered into a number of major themes, which provide the framework for the chapters of this book.

Terms are used in this book as they appeared in the records of the Georgian era, so first names are referred to as Christian names, the birth names of married women as maiden names, and illegitimate children as bastards. Although the focus of this book is the sources available for research in England, the sources for Wales are essentially the same, as England and Wales shared the same legal system and Welsh dioceses were still within the Church of England during the Georgian era. Sources for researching Jewish ancestry are not discussed, as the number of Jews in Georgian England was small and the sources are quite specialized. Extracts from original sources used as examples are not necessarily exact transcripts, as they have been edited to make them easier to read and comprehend. To avoid ambiguity, the ampersand has been used to represent the word 'and' when it occurs in proper names, such as the Diocese of Bath & Wells.

No images of original sources have been included in this book, as many of the sources used in genealogical research are quite large and do not reproduce well in black and white in books of this size, and many high-resolution images are now available online, often in colour. Furthermore, most archives now impose substantial reproduction fees for the use of images of original documents in commercially published works. DNA analysis now offers an additional tool for breaking down brick walls in the Georgian era, but is complementary to traditional research using historical sources, not a substitute for it, and is not discussed in this book.

Sources that are available online at the time of writing have been highlighted, but very specific information on how to access them is not included. The number of resources available through the major online subscription services and a wide range of other websites is constantly increasing, with web addresses (URLs) sometimes changing, so any listing of online resources will rapidly become out of date. A large proportion of online resources are available through only four online search services: Ancestry, Findmypast, The Genealogist and FamilySearch. Other websites mentioned in this book can be accessed by searching for them by name using Google. When it has been specifically mentioned that sources are not available online, this reflects the situation at the time of writing, but commercial online subscription services can be very secretive about the new resources they are planning to introduce, so significant sources can appear online quite unexpectedly.

The amount of information that can be included in a book of this size is limited, so many references are provided to books containing more detailed information about specific topics. Books of potential relevance to the wider historical context are too numerous to mention and have not been listed. The extent to which sources have been described in detail reflects their potential relevance to the average researcher. Church of England records are therefore described in greater detail than records relating to crime and punishment. This book is suitable both for readers just beginning to trace their ancestors before civil registration and for those with more experience who wish to increase their knowledge of the sources available for researching their Georgian ancestors.

Chapter 1

ASPECTS OF GENEALOGICAL RESEARCH IN GEORGIAN ENGLAND

SOURCES

Until relatively recently, the initial stages of genealogical research, involving tracing ancestors who lived during the Victorian era, could only be carried out in London. Research involved searching the large and heavy civil registration index volumes and the unindexed handwritten census schedules, only made available to the general public after a hundred years. Accessibility improved towards the end of the twentieth century with the availability of the GRO indexes on microfiche, and copies of census schedules for the areas concerned on microfilm, in archives and libraries throughout the country. Census indexes began to appear, mainly produced by volunteers in local family history societies. However, identifying the ancestors in each previous generation remained slow and laborious. Since the millennium, searching for Victorian ancestors has been transformed by online-searchable civil registration indexes and digitized and indexed census records, made available on subscription by commercial organizations. Many other relevant sources, such as digitized newspapers, are also available online. Research that might previously have taken several years can now often be carried out in days or weeks, without any need to leave home.

The reality of research before civil registration can therefore come as a sudden and unwelcome surprise to people who have become

1

accustomed to tracing their Victorian ancestors with relative ease and entirely online. Although researching Victorian ancestors is not always entirely straightforward, the rapid progress that can often be made using civil registration and census records in combination may obscure the reality that virtually none of the sources used in genealogical research today were ever intended to be used for that purpose. However, this becomes all too obvious as soon as research gets back to the early nineteenth century. Not only are fewer sources available, but they are located in a large number of different archives scattered throughout the country, and the extent to which sources have been indexed or digitized is very variable. No national system for recording births, marriages and deaths existed before 1837. Baptisms, marriages and burials were recorded in church registers, but some children were not baptized, some baptisms, marriages and burials that took place were not recorded, and not all the records that were made at the time have survived. With a few exceptions in specific areas at particular times, most church registers recorded less genealogical information than was later recorded under the civil registration system. No nationwide censuses listing individuals were taken during the Georgian era, so the places of birth of people who had died or left the country before 1851 cannot be established from census records, although this information can sometimes be found in other sources.

People are more likely to make errors in identifying their Victorian ancestors if they try to avoid buying relevant civil registration certificates and make assumptions based on the minimal information in the GRO indexes. In some cases the information in the full records tells quite a different story. Records in church registers are the main building blocks for research during the Georgian era, and making assumptions based on the minimal information they contain can also lead to errors. No corroborating evidence is available from census records, so it is necessary to search for it in other sources. The records that were made at the time that might include genealogical information reflect the social status and occupational and religious backgrounds of the individuals and families concerned. The majority of people in Georgian England were generally law-abiding and neither very prosperous nor extremely poor, but it is the people at these two extremes, and those convicted of crimes, for whom records are more likely to have been produced at the time. However, the extent to which such records have survived is often a matter of chance.

The late eighteenth century is a particularly challenging period, because the population was both increasing and becoming more mobile at a time when only minimal records were being kept. It is relatively common to encounter brick walls during this period, where individuals or families suddenly seem to appear out of nowhere. This may be an indication of migration from elsewhere, but can also be the result of deficient or defective records in the area where they had been born. Some brick walls are impossible to overcome simply because of a lack of surviving records, but it may be possible to overcome others by identifying relevant sources, searching them effectively and understanding the significance of the information they contain. Sources containing evidence of relationships between family members include apprenticeship and employment records, monumental inscriptions, wills, deeds, manorial records, records of civil disputes in the equity courts (Chancery Proceedings) and Poor Law records. In some cases the information in such records can enable relationships between two or more generations to be established even in the complete absence of church registers.

Finding genealogical information requires not only knowing what sources might be relevant, but also knowing how they can be accessed. Many books on family history describe sources in great detail, but include only superficial information about where to find them. Researchers may fail to find sources they are aware of because they were not in the places they were expecting, either in archives or online. In particular, sources for the same area, originally held by the Church of England, which are related in content, but have different custodial histories, are sometimes held in different archives. This can also affect whether and how sources can be accessed online. Although most archive websites provide detailed information about their own holdings, and often how they can be accessed online,

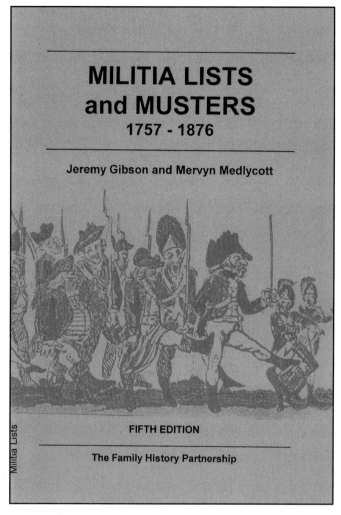

One of the 'Gibson guides' published by The Family History Partnership. These inexpensive pamphlets are an important resource for establishing the location of specific types of source, which can sometimes be held in unexpected archives.

less information may be provided on the related material available elsewhere.

Published guides to the locations of specific types of source, including the series of pamphlets available from The Family History Partnership, and commonly known as 'Gibson guides', have been available for many years. Their use is strongly recommended, but understanding the historical reasons why different sources have ended up where they are can sometimes be the key to finding elusive information. To facilitate this, Church of England sources have been grouped according to their custodial history in this book, rather than to their genealogical content. Some related sources, such as parish registers and bishop's transcripts, and marriage registers and marriage licence documents, are therefore discussed in different chapters.

THE HISTORICAL CONTEXT

The historical context within which records were created becomes increasingly relevant as research proceeds back into the past. Knowledge of a range of historical topics is necessary, mainly relating to social rather than political history. Various historical themes are particularly relevant to genealogical research in the Georgian era, including urbanization, population growth, the Industrial Revolution, the enclosure of land and long periods of war. Many of the sources now used in genealogical research were kept by churches, so some relevant background knowledge is necessary. Topics that are particularly relevant include the role of parishes, including the administration of the Poor Law, the role of the Church of England in matters such as probate, and the restrictions imposed on Protestant Nonconformists and Roman Catholics. This book includes a core of historical background necessary for researching ancestors in Georgian England, but further knowledge may be necessary when researching specific ancestors. It is particularly important to know something about the history of the area in which ancestors lived, and a wide range of books is available on researching ancestors who lived in specific areas.

Knowledge relating to ancestors' occupations and the religious denominations to which they belonged is also important. It is impossible to provide more than an outline of these topics in this book, but there are many specialist guides available. Numerous books have been published by Pen & Sword and by the Society of

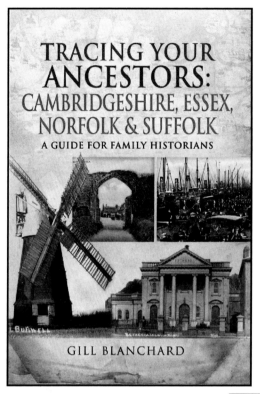

A book on researching ancestors who lived in a specific area and another on researching ancestors engaged in a specific occupation and books of this type include essential background information, as well as details of sources and where to find them.

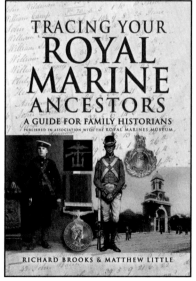

Genealogists, which describe both the sources available and their historical context.

The resemblance between the world we live in today and the world inhabited by our ancestors decreases with each previous generation, and is sometimes illusory. Students of foreign languages are warned to beware of identical words that occur in both languages but have different meanings, known as 'false friends'. The past is a foreign country in which some terms still in use today had different meanings, so false friends are also encountered in genealogical research. Coincidentally the term 'friends' is itself an example of a genealogical false friend, as it was often used in official documents in the past to refer to anyone, including family members, having a close relationship with the person concerned and not acting in any official capacity (an example of its use can be found in the settlement examination in Chapter 9). Failure to identify false friends in genealogical research can result in clues being missed and information being incorrectly interpreted.

NAMES

The spelling of surnames in the records of the Georgian era was not always consistent, particularly when the people concerned were illiterate or semi-literate, and uncommon surnames were often recorded phonetically. Variant forms of surnames are not always retrieved automatically by search systems, even when the 'search all variants' option has been selected. Many readers are likely to be familiar with this issue already as a result of researching their Victorian ancestors.

The range of Christian names in common use during the Georgian era was quite limited. Almost half the boys were named John, William or Thomas and half the girls named Mary, Elizabeth, Sarah or Ann. Middle names started to be given to children in middle-class families in the mid-eighteenth century, but only became common in lower-class families towards the end of the Georgian era. Research is often easier in families that used less common Christian names, such as Nathaniel, Laurence,

Bartholomew, Temperance, Abigail or Rebecca, or surnames used as Christian names, such as Greener or Barlow.

Uncommon Christian names were often perpetuated over several generations as a result of naming patterns, enabling ancestral lines to be established more easily. It was the tradition in many families for parents to give their children the Christian names of other family members, often in a specific order, rather than simply choosing names they liked. Many readers will already have identified Victorian ancestors and their siblings named according to such patterns. Naming patterns were even more common in the Georgian era: some families followed them rigidly, but others hardly at all. Naming practices varied between different parts of the country, from parish to parish, and among different social, religious and occupational groups. A typical example of a naming pattern is:

- First son named after the paternal grandfather.
- Second son named after the maternal grandfather.
- Third son named after the father.
- Further sons named after paternal then maternal uncles.
- First daughter named after the paternal (or maternal) grandmother.
- Second daughter named after the maternal (or paternal) grandmother.
- Third daughter named after the mother.
- Further daughters named after paternal then maternal (or maternal then paternal) aunts.

If a child died in infancy or early childhood during the Georgian era, and also for some time afterwards, it was common practice for the next child of the same sex to be born to be given the same Christian name, so a burial record for the first child can usually be found.

Adult male siblings frequently followed identical naming patterns for their own children, which often resulted in the baptisms of two or more first cousins of the same name in the same parish within a few years of each other. Because the father's name was not recorded in marriage records before 1837, identifying the correct baptism record for a bride or groom, usually but not always between twenty and thirty years before the marriage, is not always straightforward, as in the following example, in which three boys with the same name were baptized within a period of five years.

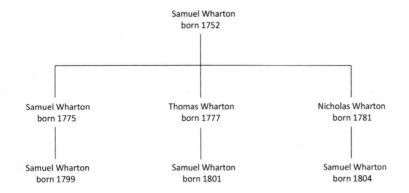

DATES

A major event during the Georgian era of significance to genealogical research was the change from the Julian to the Gregorian calendar in 1752. The Julian calendar, named after Julius Caesar, was introduced by the Romans and continued to be used until the late sixteenth century, by which time a significant discrepancy had arisen between the calendar (based on a year of 365 days with a leap year every fourth year) and the solar cycle. This resulted in incorrectly calculated dates for events such as the spring equinox, which determined the date of Easter. In 1582 the Gregorian calendar, named after Pope Gregory XIII, was introduced in much of Europe. It omitted ten days from the calendar and introduced a formula to slightly reduce the number of leap years. The Gregorian calendar was not introduced in England until 1752, when eleven days were omitted, with Wednesday 2 September being followed by Thursday 14 September. The loss of these days from the calendar can be significant in the interpretation of historical dates, but is usually ignored in genealogical research.

The change that took place in 1752 of greater significance to genealogical researchers was the change of the first day of the year from 25 March, known as Lady Day, to 1 January. Before 1752, 24 March 1746 was followed by 25 March 1747; 31 December 1747 by 1 January 1747; 24 March 1747 by 25 March 1748, and so on. Although events appear in the correct order in sources arranged chronologically, such as parish registers, with the year changing on 25 March, if dates are simply copied by researchers as they were originally recorded, events relating to dates between 1 January and 24 March can appear to have taken place the previous year. This can result in anomalies, such as the remarriage of a widower on 6 January 1736 appearing to have taken place before the death of his first wife on 28 May 1736, whereas the marriage actually took place just over seven months later on 6 January 1737 according to modern practice.

Various systems are used to avoid the potential ambiguity of pre-1752 dates. Dates recorded as they appear in original sources are sometimes referred to as *Old Style* (O.S.), with *New Style* (N.S.) indicating that the year has been adjusted to correspond to the system used today. In genealogical research, dates are often recorded using *dual dating*, with both years recorded in pre-1752 dates between 1 January and 24 March. A date recorded in an original source as 20 February 1744 would be recorded by a researcher as 20 February 1744/5. Some researchers routinely convert all pre-1752 dates they record from original sources to New Style format, but if this is done it is important to indicate that this practice has been followed when sharing information with others. Online subscription services such as Ancestry and Findmypast contain many different databases produced by a variety of organizations, and these organizations may have followed different practices when extracting and recording pre-1752 dates. However, an explanation of the practice that was followed when specific databases were produced is not always readily available. Potentially ambiguous dates found using online indexes should therefore be checked by consulting original sources or photographic facsimiles, but that is good practice in any case.

1745.

April 15. George, *s.* John and Ann Marshall, Millhouse.
Jan. 1. Margaret, *d.* John and Margaret Hakenhead, Seaham.
28. Jane, *d.* Thoms. and Barbara Whittingham, Seaham.
Feb. 16. George, *s.* John and Anne Bales, Seaton Moore.

1746.

July 28. John, *s.* John and Ann Ridley, Seaham.
Sept. 9. William, *s.* Thoms. and Isabel Reed, Seaton Moor.
Feb. 8. Mary, *d.* Robt. and Mary Mewis, Seaham.
Mar. 3. Frances, *d.* John and Ann Appleby, Seaton.

1747.

May 31. Barbara, *d.* Thomas and Barbara Whittingham, Seaham.
Aug. 16. Leolin, *s.* John and Ann Marshal, Mill house.
Sept. 27. Mary, *d.* Thomas and Isabel Reed, Seaton Moor.

1748.

April 17. Samuel, *s.* John and Margaret Hakenhead, Seaham.
17. Richard, *s.* Richard and Elisabeth Middleton, Seaham.
May 8. Thomas, *s.* Nicholas and Margart Byars, Seaton.
July 11. Henry, *s.* Robert and Jane Whitfield, Seaton.

1749.

April 9. Thomas, *s.* Thomas and Elisabeth Johnson, Seaham.

1750.

April 16. William, *s.* John and Ann Marshall, Mill House.
May 20. George, *s.* George Heaton, Seaton.
Dec. 23. Ann, *d.* Robt. and Elianor Clark, Seaham.
Jan. 1. Thomas, *s.* John and Ann Ridley, Seaham.

1751.

April 7. Mary, *d.* Matthew and Mary Stobbert, Seaton.
8. John, *s.* William and Alice Burdis, Low Sharply.
May 21. George, *s.* George and Ann Thompson, Seaton.
June 9. Jane, *d.* Nicholas and Margaret Byars, Seaton.

1752.

May 10. Henry, *s.* John and Ann Marshall, Mill House.
June 7. John, *s.* Thomas and Isabel Reed, Seaton Moor.
Nov. 26. Mary, *d.* John and Ann Ridley, Seaham.
Dec. 26. Isabel, *d.* Robert and Elianer Clark, Seaton.

1753.

Jan. 19. Edward, *s.* William and Alice Burdis, Seaton.
Aug. 5. Henry, *s.* David Linsley, Seaton.
28. Anne, *d.* George and Anne Thompson, Seaton.
Nov. 20. William, *s.* William and Frances Smith, Seaton.

A page from a transcript of a baptism register which includes the year 1752, when the first day of the year changed from 25 March to 1 January.

Further information about dates in a genealogical context can be found in Webb (1989).

HANDWRITING AND LATIN

The study of old handwriting is known as palaeography. The normal handwriting of the Georgian era is usually fairly similar to that of the twentieth century, apart from the *long s* which looks like an 'f' without a horizontal line. Both the long and short s could appear in the same word, but the short s was always used at the end of a word. The long s continued to be used to denote the first letter of a double s in handwritten documents after it had fallen out of more general use, and often well into the Victorian era. The surname Burgess, for example, would often be written as Burgeſs.

It is important for researchers to be able to read names correctly in original handwritten sources, and this can often be made easier by searching for other occurrences of letters appearing in names that are difficult to decipher in other words written in the same hand that can be more easily identified. Certain types of source, such as deeds and some wills transcribed into will registers, were written in very distinctive scripts that can be difficult to read at first. However, these

Part of a letter written in 1732. Apart from the long s, *the style is fairly similar to that of modern handwriting. The transcription is:* . . . receive you, therefore desire you[']ll come again to my house, where you were last year, w[hi]ch will be most convenient for both of Us, 'till affairs are settled, one way or another. Y[ou]r answer to Time & Place will Oblidge.

records were intended to be read by others, so the scripts used were fairly uniform, and it is possible to learn to read them with practice.

Before 1733 some legal documents and some parish register entries were written in Latin, as were some Roman Catholic registers from the late eighteenth century onwards. Some memorial inscriptions, often relating to members of the clergy or landed gentry and usually inside churches rather than in churchyards, were composed in Latin. Latin is an inflected language in which meaning is dependent on word endings and not on word order as in English. Although the Latin in many records now used in genealogical research was fairly basic, to be confident that Latin records describing relationships between individuals have been correctly interpreted requires a basic knowledge of Latin word endings.

Several books on palaeography and Latin for local and family historians are available, of which Marshall (2004) is recommended as an introduction to palaeography, and Westcott (2014) as an introduction to the Latin found in documents relevant to family history. TNA also provides excellent online tutorials on palaeography and Latin on its website. Some researchers may only rarely encounter sources containing difficult handwriting or Latin when researching their Georgian ancestors, so may prefer to rely on help from others when necessary. Archivists may be able to provide limited help (with reading specific words, for example) and many professional genealogists offer transcription and translation services.

Chapter 2

GOVERNMENT

KINGS AND KINGDOMS

The execution of Charles I in 1649 at the end of the English Civil War was followed by the Commonwealth of Oliver Cromwell. The elder son of Charles I was restored to the throne as Charles II in 1660. When Charles II died in 1685 with no legitimate children, his younger brother, who had Catholic sympathies, ascended the throne as James II. Religion at that time was not the private matter it is today, but was interwoven with politics and international relations. James II became increasingly unpopular as his reign progressed, so a plan was devised to remove him as king. James's two daughters, Mary and Anne, had been brought up as Protestants at the insistence of their uncle Charles II. In 1677 Mary, the elder daughter, had married her Protestant Dutch cousin, Prince William of Orange, and he was 'invited' to invade England in 1688 by seven members of the political establishment. William landed at Brixham in Devon with his army and marched towards London, encountering little opposition en route. James II fled to France, so was deemed to have abdicated, and William and Mary were proclaimed as the joint monarchs William III and Mary II. The virtually bloodless (in England) overthrow of James II became known as the 'Glorious Revolution'.

William and Mary had no surviving children. Mary died in 1694, and William reigned as sole monarch until his death in 1702, when Mary's younger sister Anne became queen. Anne married Prince George of Denmark in 1683 and experienced multiple pregnancies, most of which ended in miscarriage or stillbirth. Her only child to survive infancy died in 1700. The Bill of Rights of 1689 had excluded Catholics from the throne, and the Act of Settlement of 1701 anticipated what would happen after Anne's death by settling the throne on Electress Sophia of Hanover in Germany (a granddaughter of James I of England) and her Protestant descendants. Sophia died a few weeks before Anne in 1714, so her son George became George I of England. The House of Hanover now supplanted the House of Stuart and the Georgian era had begun. The Georgian era encompasses the reigns of the four Hanoverian kings named George, who reigned successively from 1714 to 1830, and is usually also considered to include the short reign of William IV from 1830 to 1837.

James II died in exile in France in 1701. As well as his two daughters by his first wife, he had a son by his second wife, named James Francis Edward Stuart, who subsequently became known as the 'Old Pretender'. His birth in 1688 had prompted the invitation to William of Orange to invade England. Supporters of James II and his successors were known as Jacobites, and consisted largely of Roman Catholics and Anglican Tories. Jacobitism was strongest in northern Scotland, but was also strong in some areas of northern England. Following the accession of George I, a Jacobite rising took place in 1715 with the aim of restoring the Old Pretender to the throne. The rising was concentrated in Scotland, but a Jacobite force marched into England and was defeated at Preston in Lancashire. Thirty years later, in 1745, the Old Pretender's son, Charles Edward Stuart, known as 'The Young Pretender' and also as 'Bonnie Prince Charlie', landed in Scotland and raised a Jacobite army, which defeated the British army at Prestonpans near Edinburgh, marched into England and captured Carlisle. The army reached Derby, but in the absence of expected support from English Jacobites and the French, retreated to Scotland. The Jacobite army was finally defeated at Culloden, near Inverness, in April 1746. Although riots and civil disturbances were a regular occurrence during the Georgian era, no major threats to the Hanoverian dynasty occurred after 1746.

The dates of the reigns of kings and queens are of some significance to family history researchers because dates in many records appear in a form that includes the year of the king's reign, known as the *regnal year*. Although the calendar year was also included in most official documents of this period, the regnal year can provide useful confirmation when the calendar year is unclear or illegible. The years of the reigns of the Georgian kings are as follows:

1714–27	George I
1727–60	George II (son of George I)
1760–1820	George III (grandson of George II)
1820–30	George IV (son of George III)
1830–7	William IV (son of George III)

George III suffered short bouts of mental illness in 1788–89, 1801 and 1804, from which he recovered, but became permanently ill in 1810. His son George, Prince of Wales, acted as regent from 1811 until his father's death in 1820. Although the Regency only lasted for nine years, the description 'Regency era' is often used to describe a longer period from the mid-1790s to the mid-1820s. The period between the Glorious Revolution of 1688 and the Great Reform Act of 1832 (discussed below), is sometimes referred to by historians as the 'long eighteenth century'.

England began the Georgian era as part of the Kingdom of Great Britain and ended it as part of the United Kingdom of Great Britain and Ireland. In a geographical context the descriptions 'Great Britain' and 'Ireland' refer to the two major islands of the British Isles, but these terms have also been used to refer to specific kingdoms. The Kingdom of England was established before the Norman Conquest, and England remained a separate kingdom until 1707, with Wales becoming part of the kingdom during the sixteenth century. In 1603 James VI of Scotland became King of England as James I, but England and Scotland remained separate kingdoms until they were united into the Kingdom of Great Britain by the Act of Union of 1707. Scotland was sometimes referred to in records as 'North Britain' and England and Wales less frequently as 'South Britain'.

Henry VIII was proclaimed King of Ireland in the sixteenth century, and the Kingdom of Ireland was ruled by English monarchs until 1800. By the Acts of Union of 1800, which came into effect in 1801, the kingdoms of Great Britain and Ireland were united as the United Kingdom of Great Britain and Ireland. The term 'Great Britain'

King George III, who reigned for almost half of the Georgian era, from 1760 to 1820.

can therefore refer both to the geographical land mass and to the kingdom that existed from 1707 to 1800.

From the fourteenth century until 1800 English monarchs also claimed the throne of France. Records used by genealogical researchers, such as wills and deeds, frequently contain dates that include the regnal year and the names of the relevant kingdoms, for example:

> on the ninth day of June, in the year of Our Lord 1768, in the eighth year of the reign of Our Sovereign Lord George the Third, by the grace of God, of Great Britain, France and Ireland, King, Defender of the Faith, &c.

Documents after 1801 usually refer to the king 'of the United Kingdom of Great Britain and Ireland', but some printed forms containing the reference to France continued to be used until well into the nineteenth century.

PARLIAMENT

Following the Glorious Revolution of 1688, the Bill of Rights of 1689 limited the power of the monarch and established the supremacy of Parliament, although monarchs continued to hold considerable power throughout the Georgian era. As is still the case today, Parliament consisted of two Houses: the House of Lords and the House of Commons. The House of Lords consisted of hereditary peers and the bishops. Despite its name, the House of Commons was not an assembly of the common people, but of men who were almost all either the sons of peers or substantial landowners, and who were elected by a relatively small number of voters who were almost all landowners.

Voting was public, so voters were subject to bribery and coercion. Each county elected two MPs known as *Knights of the Shire,* and some boroughs also elected two MPs known as *Burgesses*. Most of these boroughs had been given this right in the Middle Ages, when the population distribution of the country had been quite different. Voting in parliamentary elections was dependent on the ownership of property in counties and on a range of criteria in cities and boroughs. By the eighteenth century some borough constituencies had become 'pocket boroughs', in which voters were in the pocket of a local landowner, often because they were his tenants, and dutifully returned him or his nominee. Others were 'rotten boroughs', with a very small number of electors who could be persuaded or bribed to vote for a particular candidate. In the early nineteenth century, for example, Old Sarum in Wiltshire, containing three houses and seven voters, returned two MPs, whereas large towns such as Manchester and Birmingham, which had grown during the eighteenth century, returned none.

Agitation for parliamentary reform, mainly from the middle class, developed towards the end of the eighteenth century, but was stifled during the wars with France between 1793 and 1815.

The House of Commons. Despite its name, MPs were almost all prosperous landowners.

The Tory governments in power from 1815 to 1830 were opposed to reform, but following the election of a Whig government in 1830, the Great Reform Act came into effect in 1832. Many of the more serious defects of the electoral system were resolved, but the number of voters only increased by about 50 per cent. The electorate now included most middle-class men, and although not as radical as many people had hoped, the Great Reform Act was the first step in a gradual process of electoral reform, culminating in universal adult suffrage, which took almost a century to achieve.

Sheriffs of counties and mayors of boroughs kept records of voters, their abodes, and the candidates they voted for, which were often published as *poll books*. Original poll books are held in local archives, but many have been digitized or transcribed and can be found online. Voters in counties comprised owners of land worth forty shillings. The breadth of the franchise in boroughs varied, and in some towns and cities included tradesmen, such as shoemakers, tailors and bakers, whose occupations were often recorded. Poll books may therefore enable a man's occupation to be established when not recorded in parish registers or other sources. Poll books known to exist are listed by county in Gibson and Rogers (2008).

Between 1780 and 1832 Land Tax assessments (discussed in the following section) were used to determine the eligibility to vote. From 1832, *electoral registers* were published, listing men's names, abodes and qualification to vote. Electoral registers are held in local archives and some are held at the British Library (BL) in London. Electoral registers from 1832 to 1932 held at the BL have been digitized and indexed by Findmypast, but coverage before 1885 is modest. Some collections held locally, including those for London, are also available online.

NATIONAL GOVERNMENT

Government in Georgian England can be characterised as 'small government'. Most of the services provided by central government today were either provided locally, such as poor relief, or not provided at all. The areas of government that impinged on the lives of ordinary people were raising revenue through taxation, defence of the realm and the legal system. The major expenditure of government was the army and navy, so defence and taxation were inextricably linked, with taxation increasing during wartime.

The government collected revenue through taxation, with different systems in operation at different times. *Land Tax* was collected from the late seventeenth century until the twentieth. Comprehensive collections of records for the Georgian era exist for a few areas, such as the City of London, but for many counties records only survive for the period from the 1770s to 1832, when they were used to establish the right to vote. These records are held with Quarter Sessions records in local archives. Land Tax records included the names of owners and occupiers, but occupiers of small properties were not necessary listed individually. Some Land Tax assessments have been transcribed and may be available online, and those for some counties have been digitized.

From 1798 owners were able to redeem the Land Tax by a payment of fifteen years' tax, although their names continued to be listed in the annual assessments for electoral purposes. An enumeration of all owners and occupiers liable to the tax was carried out in 1798. These records are held at TNA in series IR 23 *Land Tax Redemption Office: Quotas and Assessments* and have been digitized and indexed by Ancestry. Properties valued at under 20 shillings (£1) per year were exempted from Land Tax after 1798, which may explain why some people cannot be found in these records.

Land Tax records contain no genealogical information, but a continuous set of records can sometimes be used in combination with parish registers to enable relationships between individuals to be confirmed. The disappearance of a name from Land Tax assessments may be followed by the appearance of another individual with the same surname, such as a widow or eldest son. This can enable burial records before 1813, when age at death was not routinely recorded, to be correlated with deaths of individuals. Land Tax records may also enable the migration of an individual from one parish to another at a particular time to be confirmed.

A *window tax* was also imposed throughout the Georgian era, but the surviving records are scantier. Some records survive in Quarter Sessions, parish, borough and city records, and some lists of taxpayers have been published. Surviving land and window tax assessments are listed in Gibson et al. (2004).

Duties were imposed on various goods, both home-produced and imported. Home-produced goods were subject to Excise Duty, administered by the Board of Excise. Many imported goods were subject to Customs Duty, administered by the Board of Customs. These duties were collected by Customs and Excise officers, and records of the Boards of Customs and Excise, discussed in Chapter 6, can enable officers' careers to be investigated.

Stamp Duty was imposed on a variety of goods and services during the Georgian era. The Stamp Duty on newspapers gradually increased, before being substantially reduced in 1836 and finally abolished in 1855. Newspapers were therefore mainly the preserve of the middle and upper classes during the Georgian era. From 1711 to 1811, Stamp Duty was levied on apprenticeship indentures, and the records that were kept are discussed in Chapter 6. Stamp Duty was imposed on entries in parish registers from 1783 to 1794, although paupers were exempt, with the result that some parents did not have their children baptized during this period.

Several different taxes were introduced at the end of the eighteenth century to pay for the wars with France, including income tax from 1799 to 1802. An annual Stamp Duty on the wearing of hair powder was introduced in 1795, and lists of those who paid, mainly men from the middle and upper classes, were kept by the Clerk of the Peace (the clerk to the court of Quarter Sessions). These lists have often survived in collections of Quarter Sessions records, available in local archives, and the lists for some areas have been published. Death Duty was introduced in 1796. Most wills and administrations attracted Death Duty, and the records that were kept are discussed in Chapter 4.

The government was responsible for the army and navy, and for the militia when it was 'embodied' during wartime. A huge amount of information has survived for the Georgian era and is held at TNA. Sources relevant to researching soldiers, sailors, marines, Royal Dockyard employees and militiamen are discussed in Chapter 7.

Most crimes were tried by Justices of the Peace (magistrates) at Petty Sessions or Quarter Sessions. More serious crimes were tried by judges at Assize courts. The courts of equity (Chancery and Exchequer) enabled people to attempt to resolve civil disputes, often in connection with land, trusts, wills, inheritance and breach of contract. The counties of Durham, Lancashire and Cheshire were *palatinates* until the early nineteenth century, and had a degree of independence from national government, holding their own Assize and equity courts. Court records are discussed in Chapter 11.

LOCAL GOVERNMENT

Counties

Counties were established during the Anglo-Saxon period. Their boundaries hardly changed from the end of the Middle Ages until the Victorian era and their functions in local government remained essentially the same. The Lord Lieutenant in each county, usually a member of the aristocracy, was responsible for defence. The High Sheriff, usually a member of the untitled landed gentry, was appointed on an annual basis and had a variety of administrative responsibilities.

Until county councils were established in 1889, counties were governed by the Justices of the Peace of each county meeting at Quarter Sessions. Minor administrative matters were dealt with at Petty Sessions. The administrative responsibilities of Justices of the Peace included maintenance of bridges and supervision of the Poor Law. The majority of counties in England were divided into areas known as *hundreds*, but in counties that had previously been under Viking influence, including Yorkshire (subdivided into North, West and East Ridings) and Lincolnshire, such areas were known as *wapentakes*. County subdivisions were known as *wards* in the four northern counties of Cumberland, Westmorland, Northumberland and Durham, *rapes* in Sussex and *lathes* in Kent. Hundreds and their equivalents had little or no administrative power, but were often used as geographical subdivisions in various aspects of county administration, so some collections of records are arranged by hundred. Each hundred or equivalent had a High Constable, appointed on a yearly basis, responsible to the Justices of the Peace within the hundred. County records are described in detail in Raymond (2016).

Cities and Boroughs

Many cities and towns had been granted a degree of autonomy from the county in which they were geographically situated before the Georgian era, including the right to appoint their own Justices of the Peace. Boroughs were often controlled by corporations, usually comprising merchants and master craftsmen, which sometimes controlled apprenticeships and admitted men as freemen. Most of the smaller boroughs were abolished following the Municipal Corporations Act of 1835, and many new boroughs were established in populous areas.

During the Georgian era 'London' as a unit of local government referred to the City of London. All parishes outside this very small area (sometimes referred to as 'the square mile') were in the separate counties of Middlesex, Essex, Kent and Surrey.

Parishes

English parishes were involved in various aspects of local government. Each parish had a 'council' known as the *Vestry*, named after the room in the church where it usually met, which had responsibility for both ecclesiastical and civil matters. The Vestry appointed parish officers, including Churchwardens and Overseers of the Poor, who were usually unpaid. Parish officers performing their civil duties were responsible not to the archdeacon or bishop but to the Justices of the Peace of the county. The records kept by parishes did not necessarily make a distinction between civil and ecclesiastical matters, and are discussed together in Chapter 3.

Administratively a parish was part of a hundred, or its equivalent, within a county. Information in county records relating to the civil functions of parishes is usually found in Petty Sessions and Quarter Sessions records. The main civil function of parishes was in connection with the Poor Law, which is discussed in Chapter 9.

Some large parishes, particularly in the north of England, were subdivided into smaller areas known as townships, each of which had its own Overseers. In the south of England, larger parishes were often divided into tithings, which originated as subdivisions of manors (discussed below). Some large parishes were divided into quarters for the collection of rates.

Parish Constables were appointed annually and had a variety of duties, including controlling civil disturbances, making arrests, evicting vagrants and escorting paupers being removed to their parish of settlement. They were sometimes referred to as Petty Constables to distinguish them from the High Constables of hundreds. Subdivisions of larger parishes, each with its own Constable, were sometimes known as Constablewicks or Constabularies.

The Local Government Act of 1894 transferred the civil functions of Vestries to parish councils in rural areas and to town and city councils in urban areas. Ownership of historical civil records also passed to these councils, but in practice they often remained in churches, particularly in rural areas. Many records, not perceived to be of any lasting value at the time, are known or believed to have been disposed of in waste paper salvage drives during the two world wars. As a result of boundary changes and the designation of certain archives as diocesan record offices, surviving civil parish records are sometimes now held in different archives to ecclesiastical records for the same parish, although there may be some duplication on microfilm. Ecclesiastical and civil parish records are more likely to be held in different archives in urban areas, such as Greater London, the West Midlands, South and West Yorkshire, Greater Manchester, Merseyside, Tyneside and Wearside.

Manors

During the Middle Ages all land belonged to the king under the feudal system and was divided into manors. The freehold of each manor was held by a landlord, who could be an individual or a corporate body. A man who held the lordship of a manor was not necessarily titled, but if untitled usually assumed the social rank of 'Esquire' and was known locally as the 'squire'. Some manorial lordships were held by corporate bodies, such as deans and chapters of cathedrals, and colleges of the universities of Oxford and Cambridge. The Lord of the Manor often farmed some of the land himself and let the remainder to tenants, who either rendered services or paid money as rent. Rendering services gradually died out and paying rent was the norm by the Georgian era.

Some manors had the same or similar boundaries to parishes, but there could be several manors within a parish, or several parishes within a manor. A manor could consist of a single area or several separate areas of land. Some manorial lordships included patronage of the local parish church, with the right to appoint the incumbent. The manor house and church were often adjacent in such parishes. Manors could be bought and sold, and the history of the ownership of manors can often be found in the *Victoria County History* for the relevant county. Published volumes can usually be found in archives or local studies libraries and some sections are available online.

Manor courts were held both to record the transfer of land (the Court Baron) and for the maintenance of law and order (the Court Leet), but by the Georgian era the latter responsibility had largely passed to Parish Constables and Justices of the Peace. Manor courts were presided over by stewards who were usually lawyers. Some towns and villages were manorial boroughs in which vestiges of the earlier system, such as the Court Leet, persisted into the Georgian era.

During the Middle Ages manors were divided into tithings of about ten households, with one man in each, known as a Tithingman, responsible for the behaviour of its members. By the beginning of the Georgian era this responsibility had largely passed to Parish Constables appointed by Vestries, but some manorial courts continued to appoint Tithingmen. The subdivisions of some parishes continued to be referred to as tithings, with the Constables in those areas referred to as Tithingmen.

The main function of manorial courts in the Georgian era was the transfer of land, which is discussed in Chapter 10.

Chapter 3

PARISHES

The Church of England played a much more significant role in the lives of our Georgian ancestors than it does today, and was responsible for keeping many of the records now used in family history research. Its structure and hierarchical organization are therefore of considerable significance to genealogical research before 1837. The records relating to each parish and its inhabitants can be divided into three categories:

- Records kept by the parish as the smallest unit of the Church of England, being responsible to the local archdeacon or bishop, such as parish registers and Churchwardens' accounts (discussed in this chapter).
- Records kept by the parish in its civil role, being responsible to the local Justices of the Peace, such as records of the Overseers of the Poor (the Poor Law is discussed in Chapter 9).
- Records kept by higher levels of the church hierarchy, such as bishop's transcripts, marriage licence bonds and allegations and probate records (discussed in Chapter 4).

Identifying both the physical location and online availability of specific types of record relating to relevant parishes can be crucial to overcoming brick walls during the Georgian era. As was mentioned in the previous chapter, the ecclesiastical and civil functions of parishes were separated in 1894, so ecclesiastical and civil records for the same parish are sometimes now held in two different archives, particularly in urban areas. Furthermore, the boundaries of present-day counties and dioceses are quite different to those of the Georgian era, so records that are related to each other, such as marriage registers and marriage licence records, can sometimes be held in different archives.

THE GEORGIAN PARISH

The size of parishes in Georgian England varied considerably. Most parish boundaries had been established during the Middle Ages when the density of population in the south of England was much higher than in the north. Southern parishes often covered only a few square miles and sometimes considerably less. The City of London had many small parishes consisting of only a few streets, as did some other cities, such as Norwich, which had over thirty parishes. At the opposite end of the scale, the largest parish in England, Whalley in Lancashire, covered 161 square miles.

Chapels serving specific areas within parishes, and licensed for baptisms, marriages and burials, were known as *parochial chapelries*, and in most respects functioned as if they were separate parishes. They usually became parishes in their own right in the nineteenth century. Additional chapels known as *chapels of ease* were built as places of worship in larger parishes. Baptisms, marriages and burials generally took place at the main parish church, although some chapels of ease were licensed for baptisms. Some areas known as *extra-parochial places* were outside the jurisdiction of any parish, so their inhabitants did not pay church rates or poor rates, and baptisms, marriages and burials were performed in neighbouring parishes. Some parishes or groups of parishes, known as *peculiars*, lay within the geographical boundaries of a diocese but were not under the jurisdiction of its bishop. Peculiars were under a variety of other jurisdictions, including bishops of other dioceses and deans and chapters of cathedrals. Most extra-parochial places and peculiars were abolished during the Victorian era.

By the early nineteenth century accommodation in many parish churches was totally inadequate, particularly in the newly-industrialized areas in the Midlands and north, where churches were often dominated by private pew-holders. Not only were many churches extremely overcrowded, but there were no Anglican churches at all in many new settlements situated in what had previously been large and sparsely-populated parishes. Relatively few new Anglican churches were built before the end of the wars with France in 1815, but this situation changed following the Church Building Act of 1818. The term *ancient parish* is not precisely defined, but is often used to refer to those parishes that were in existence when the Church of England was established by Henry VIII. Because so few new parishes had been created in the intervening period, in 1820 almost all parishes were still ancient parishes, but this changed rapidly in densely-populated areas. When new churches were built, new parishes were created and existing parish boundaries were revised, so children were sometimes baptized at a different parish church to their older siblings even though the family were still living in the same house.

The profession of Church of England clergyman was more of a career than a calling during the Georgian era. Most clergymen were from middle- and upper-class backgrounds and had been educated at Oxford or Cambridge. The principal clergyman of a parish was the *incumbent,* who held the *benefice* or *living* for life. The right to appoint the incumbent (subject to the bishop's approval) was known as the *advowson,* and was in the hands of the *patron,* who was often a member of the local landed gentry. The advowson was a form of property that could be bought, sold or inherited. Squire and parson were often related in rural parishes, with members of the same family occupying the manor house and the rectory or vicarage, which were sometimes adjacent.

The incumbent was designated as a *rector, vicar* or *perpetual curate,* depending on the historical right to receive tithes. Some incumbents were assisted by one or more *curates,* who could be young clergymen waiting to obtain livings of their own or older clergymen unable to obtain them, as obtaining a living was often dependent on influence and family connections. Well-connected clergymen could be appointed as incumbents of more than one parish, sometimes a considerable distance apart, a practice known as *pluralism.* They could reside where they chose, and often chose to reside in the parish closest to the family 'seat', employing curates to serve the parishes in which they did not reside. In the early nineteenth century, for example, John Fellowes, a younger son from a family of Norfolk gentry, was simultaneously rector of Bramerton, vicar of Easton, rector of Mautby and rector of Shotesham, all in Norfolk, and rector of Bratton Clovelly in Devon, some 350 miles away. Over half of all incumbents were non-resident at the beginning of the nineteenth century.

Anglican clergymen, even poorly-paid curates, generally moved within the same social sphere as the local gentry, and it was not uncommon for clergymen who were the sons of yeomen or master craftsmen to marry into local landowning families. From the mid-eighteenth century until well into the Victorian era a proportion of clergymen were Justices of the Peace, with one incumbent in six acting as a magistrate in the early nineteenth century. There was much poverty and social unrest in the late eighteenth and early nineteenth centuries, and the existence of so many parson magistrates is likely to have increased the antipathy of many lower-class families towards the Church of England.

Parishes were governed by Vestries, as mentioned in Chapter 2. Churchwardens (or Chapelwardens in parochial chapelries) were responsible to the archdeacon and bishop for the maintenance of the church building and had various functions in connection with church services. They collected church rates, agreed by the Vestry, to cover the necessary expenses. Churchwardens were also responsible for the moral and religious life of parishes, but their influence in this respect gradually declined as the Georgian age progressed. The Churchwardens and other parish officers such as the Overseers of the Poor had responsibilities relating to the civil functions of the parish, for which they were responsible to the local Justices of the Peace rather than the church authorities. Each parish had a Parish Clerk, who was a layman with a variety of responsibilities for which he received payment. Unlike Churchwardens and Overseers, who were appointed annually, Parish Clerks often served for many years, and it was not uncommon for the position to pass from father to son.

Parish registers were supposed to be stored in a locked chest, originally of wood but later of iron, known as the parish chest, which was also used for the storage of other parish records, both ecclesiastical and civil. The range of records that might have been found in a parish chest many years ago are described in the classic book by Tate (1969), first published in 1946 when most parish records were still held in churches. The term 'parish chest material' is sometimes used to refer to miscellaneous parish records other than parish registers, the survival of which can vary from parish to parish. Raymond (2015) provides an overview of all types of parish record.

PARISH REGISTERS

Rather than recording births, deaths and marriages as under the civil registration system, parish registers recorded baptisms, marriages and burials. Before 1813 the instructions to clergy were that parish registers were to be written up each Sunday after divine service by the clergyman in the presence of the Churchwardens, but these instructions were often ignored. Parish registers had to be written up in ink, but in the days of quill pens it was common practice to keep a rough register written in pencil, or to write entries on slips of paper, and to copy up the entries into the parish register at intervals. In some parishes the registers were written up by the Parish Clerk rather than the clergyman.

Separate baptism, marriage and burial registers were kept in some parishes throughout the Georgian era, particularly in more populous parishes in urban areas. Before 1754, the baptisms, marriages and burials in many smaller parishes were recorded in a single volume, either interspersed in a single chronological sequence, in separate columns, on separate pages, or in separate sections. Hardwicke's Marriage Act (discussed below) required separate marriage registers to be kept from 1754, but baptisms and burials often continued to be recorded in the same volume until separate printed registers were introduced in 1813.

At the beginning of the Georgian era most parish registers recorded only minimal information. This could sometimes cause difficulties for people who needed to prove their identity or confirm their relationship to others, such as when trying to establish their right to inherit land or property. In 1764, Ralph Bigland, a Herald of the College of Arms, antiquarian and genealogist, wrote the first book to be published about parish registers. Entitled *Observations on*

Marriages, Baptisms and Burials as Preserved in Parochial Registers, it made specific recommendations for more genealogical information to be included in parish registers than hitherto. It seems likely that it was the publication of this book that encouraged some clergymen to subsequently record more information in their parish registers and some bishops to request or require the incumbents in their dioceses to do likewise. However, a considerable variation in the amount of detail recorded in parish registers continued until 1813.

From 1783 to 1794 a Stamp Duty of threepence (3d = 1.25p) was imposed on every birth, baptism, marriage or burial entry in parish registers, but paupers were exempt. Evidence suggests that some clergymen who were sympathetic to the plight of those poorer parishioners not receiving parish relief either recorded them as paupers or paid the fees out of their own pockets. Some registers were annotated to indicate who had paid and who was exempt: for example *Pd*, short for paid, denoted payment of the tax and *P* denoted a pauper. Separate, printed, baptism and burial registers were introduced in some parishes following the imposition of Stamp Duty.

At the beginning of 1813 *An Act for the Better Regulating and Preserving of Parish and Other Registers of Births, Baptisms, Marriages and Burials in England* came into effect. It is commonly known as 'Rose's Act', after George Rose, the MP who introduced the legislation. Standardized printed baptism, marriage and burial registers were introduced, with clear guidance on what information was to be recorded. The relatively modest requirements of Rose's Act were an extremely watered-down version of the original proposals, which if they had been implemented would undoubtedly have resulted in many fewer headaches for subsequent generations of genealogical researchers.

Peaks and troughs in the number of baptisms, marriages and burials from year to year in a single parish might occur for a variety of valid reasons, but any large decrease in the number of recorded events is worthy of further investigation. Evidence can sometimes be found that no events, or very few, were recorded in parish registers for periods of weeks, months or even years. Although such gaps can often be identified using indexes and transcripts, other signs of neglect can only be observed by examining images of the original handwritten registers. A register in which very few entries were made over a prolonged period may include a few entries that must have been written in later, often in different handwriting. In other cases, it may be evident from the handwriting that several months or years must have been written up retrospectively on a single occasion by the same person. This can give the illusion of accuracy and completeness, but any set of records compiled from earlier notes is prone to copying errors and may suffer from omissions. Obvious errors in copying can sometimes be identified, and evidence can sometimes be found from other sources indicating that events not recorded in parish registers almost certainly took place.

Steel (1976) provides a very comprehensive history of parish registers including a detailed account of the reasons why some no longer survive or are defective. As mentioned above, many parishes did not have resident incumbents but were served by curates, who themselves might not be resident, and registers were often left in the care of Parish Clerks. Some parish registers for some or all of the Georgian era no longer survive. The reasons include neglect, fire, flood, and the destruction of churches and their registers in air raids during the Second World War. Deficiencies in, or the loss of, parish registers can sometimes be made up, in whole or in part, by bishop's transcripts and any other printed, typescript or manuscript copies that had been produced from the original registers. Searching for records of baptisms, marriages and burials is discussed in Chapter 13.

The majority of historical parish records continued to be kept in churches until well into the twentieth century. However, following the Parochial Registers and Records Measure of 1978, specific archives were designated as diocesan record offices for the deposit of ecclesiastical parish records. Churches were permitted to hold their own historical records if certain conditions were met, and only a very small number chose to do so. Except when still held by churches, historical parish registers and other ecclesiastical parish records have been deposited in local archives. However, baptism and burial registers begun in 1813 in very sparsely populated parishes may still be held by incumbents if they have not yet been filled up.

The current location of historical parish records is not always obvious, and is dependent on both county and diocesan boundaries. For example, the records of parishes now in the Diocese of Liverpool, but which were within the county of Lancashire and Diocese of Chester during the Georgian era, are held at Liverpool Record Office, Lancashire Archives and Wigan Archives. Records of those parishes in Teesdale that were in the North Riding of Yorkshire before 1974 but are now in Co. Durham, such as Romaldkirk and Bowes, are held at Durham County Record Office. Documents from the Georgian era refer to these parishes as being in the North Riding of Yorkshire, so it might be assumed that the parish registers would now be held at North Yorkshire County Record Office in Northallerton, and be included in digitized collections of Yorkshire parish registers now available online, but neither of these assumptions is correct.

The physical location of parish records can therefore affect whether they have been digitized. It is particularly relevant to accessing records other than parish registers (discussed later in this chapter), which are less likely to have been digitized, and have rarely been indexed by name. Establishing the whereabouts and online availability of parish records, particularly those close to county boundaries, is vital to ensure that all parishes in an area have been covered. *The Phillimore Atlas and Index of Parish Registers*, edited by Cecil Humphery-Smith (2003), includes an extremely useful collection of coloured county maps showing the locations of parishes, including peculiars, within the ecclesiastical boundaries that existed in 1832. It is often available for consultation in libraries and archive searchrooms. Larger-scale versions of the county maps from this volume are available for purchase from the Institute of Heraldic and Genealogical Studies (IHGS) in Canterbury, and the maps have also been digitized by Ancestry. Similar maps may be available from local archives and family history societies.

The *National Index of Parish Registers* was begun by the Society of Genealogists in the 1960s, with the aim of producing detailed county listings, and volumes for many counties were published. Information on the availability of parish registers is usually now available on

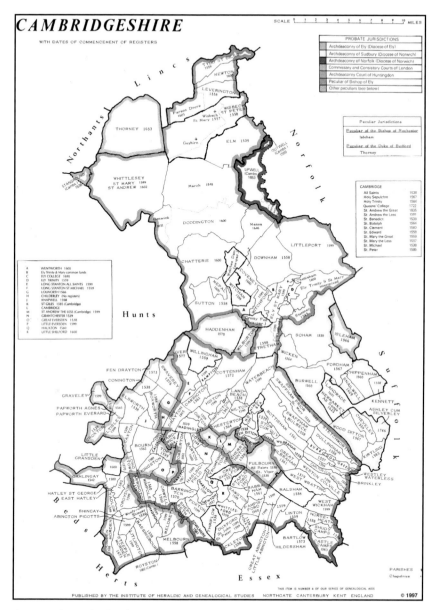

A map of Cambridgeshire from the The Phillimore Atlas and Index of Parish
Registers *(reproduced with permission of the Trustees and Principal of the Institute
of Heraldic and Genealogical Studies, Northgate, Canterbury. www.ihgs.ac.uk).*

archive websites, but these volumes, which are often available in archives and local studies libraries, can still be useful.

Towards the end of the twentieth century, parish registers were routinely made available to archive users as microfilm copies, to avoid the further wear and tear to the originals that would have resulted from their continuing use by a growing number of family history researchers. Since the millennium the parish registers held in some archives have been digitized and made available online, and the number of digitized collections continues to grow. Digital images of many record collections have been produced by digitizing existing black-and-white microfilms, but the original parish registers in some archives have been re-photographed in colour, which can often enable them to be read more easily.

Most collections of digitized parish registers are available through online search services such as Ancestry, Findmypast, The Genealogist and FamilySearch, but some, such as those for Essex and the Medway area of Kent, are available on separate websites. Many parish registers have been indexed, but without links to images. The *FamilySearch Wiki* includes information on the availability of indexes and digitized images for individual parishes, and the *GENUKI* website provides detailed information for some counties.

Baptism Registers

Most children were baptized publicly in church, usually on Sundays, but occasionally on other days if they were not expected to live. It was normal practice at the beginning of the Georgian era for children to be baptized on the first or second Sunday after birth, but the average interval between birth and baptism increased after 1760, particularly in some urban areas. Children could also be baptized at home, referred to as a *private baptism*. Although this was intended to be carried out only in exceptional circumstances, such as when a child's life was in danger, evidence suggests that private baptism as a matter of course became much more widespread towards the end of the eighteenth century, particularly in London. Children could not be baptized twice, but parents who had a child baptized privately, sometimes referred to as being *half baptized*, were expected to bring the child to church on a Sunday to be *received into the church*. Two entries on different dates can therefore sometimes be found in baptism registers for children who had been privately baptized, the first relating to a private baptism, sometimes abbreviated as *P.B.* and the second to being received into the church, sometimes abbreviated as *Rec'd*. Although no distinction was made between the terms 'baptism' and 'christening' in the canons of the Church of England, some clergymen appear to have used the term christening to refer to reception into the church as distinct from baptism, the sacrament of anointing with holy water. Records in baptism registers can occasionally be found referring to children being 'baptized and christened' on the same day, and sometimes on different days in different parishes. For example, the following record appears in the baptism register of Hayton in Cumberland on 15 December 1789:

> Adam son of Ann Parker of Brampton, Spinster, illegitimate – christened, being baptised at Brampton

Most children were baptized as infants, but some late and adult baptisms took place. Records of late baptisms often included either the date of birth or the age at baptism, but there are many instances where a late baptism must have taken place, although neither date of birth nor age were recorded. The imposition of Stamp Duty on entries in parish registers from 1783 to 1794 particularly affected baptisms. Evidence suggests that some parents living in populous parishes who were not regular churchgoers did not have their children baptized during this period, although some of these children may have been baptized after the tax was withdrawn. Siblings born between 1783 and 1794 were sometimes baptized together afterwards.

Before 1813 there was no standard format for entries in baptism registers, and the amount of information recorded varied, both from parish to parish, and in a single parish over a period of time. It was not uncommon for the baptism record of a child to include only the date of baptism, the name of the child and the name of the father, so an entry might appear as:

> 3 September 1747   John the son of John Smith

However, the mother's Christian name was included in a significant proportion of baptism records during the Georgian era, for example:

10 June 1781   William the son of John and Mary Smith

Place of abode was sometimes recorded in the registers of larger parishes, particularly in the north of England. Birthplace was sometimes noted when a child had not been born in the parish. The father's occupation was recorded in some parishes during specific periods and was sometimes noted if the parents were temporary residents, such as when the father was a soldier or serving in the militia, in which case the name of the regiment was often recorded. From the late 1760s the date of birth as well as the date of baptism was routinely recorded in some registers. The printed baptism registers used in some parishes from 1783 made provision for recording the date of birth as well as the date of baptism.

More detailed registers were kept, on the initiative of individual incumbents, in parishes scattered around the country, although their successors sometimes abandoned the practice. One of the earliest examples is the baptism register of Colyton in Devon between 1765 and 1778, in which the name of the mother's father was recorded. The recording of this information came to an end in 1778, following a change of incumbent. Few such registers were introduced at the instigation of incumbents, but they were either encouraged or required by the bishops of some dioceses. As well as the date of birth, the mother's maiden name, the father's occupation and the parents' abode were frequently recorded in baptism registers of parishes in the Diocese of Carlisle from about 1770, and the mother's maiden name in baptism registers of parishes in the Diocese of Norwich from 1783.

The amount of genealogical information recorded in parish registers in the dioceses of York and Durham went a stage further. In 1777 the Archbishop of York, William Markham, instructed clergy in the Diocese of York to follow the recommendations of a local clergyman, William Dade. The registers that were subsequently introduced are now referred to as Dade registers.

Entries in baptism registers include the name, the dates of birth and baptism of the child, the seniority (1st son, 2nd son, etc.), the father's name, abode, and occupation, the name of the father's father (and sometimes the names of the father's mother and her father) and abode, and the name of the mother and her father (and sometimes the names of the mother's mother and her father) and abode. A typical entry in a Dade baptism register, from Fishlake, near Doncaster, in 1786, is:

> William Ward, born 12 August, baptised 13 August, First child of John Ward, carpenter, son of John Ward of Fulnetby in the County of Lincoln, farmer, by Ann his wife, daughter of William Bingham of Morton in the parish of Gainsborough, miller.

Many clergymen were resistant to the new system because of the extra work involved in recording such a large amount of additional information, particularly in populous areas, and the Archbishop was apparently unwilling to enforce it. Although the Dade system was followed in many Yorkshire parishes until the new printed registers were introduced in 1813 (discussed below), in other parishes it was abandoned, adopted only partially or not adopted at all. The Diocese of York included the Archdeaconry of Nottingham, so Dade registers exist for some Nottinghamshire parishes. Some clergymen elsewhere in England seem to have been impressed by the Dade system, and adopted it in their own parishes. An example is Branscombe in Devon, where the baptism records from 1794 to 1812 are very full and include the names and abodes of both sets of grandparents.

In 1798, the Bishop of Durham, Shute Barrington, introduced a slightly less detailed system in the Diocese of Durham, which was followed in almost all parishes in Northumberland and Co. Durham. A typical Barrington baptism record included the name of the child and dates of birth and baptism, the seniority (1st son, 2nd son, etc.), the father's name, abode, occupation and birthplace, and the mother's maiden name and birthplace (and sometimes her father's name). An example from a typical Barrington baptism register, from Ebchester in Co. Durham, is:

> Margaret Gibson, Broad Oak, born 14 June 1803, baptised 3 July 1803, 3rd daughter of George Gibson, tailor, of Whitburn by his wife Ann Stephenson native of Milkwellburn, Ovingham parish, Northumberland.

Barrington and Dade registers were continued for several years after 1812 in a few parishes, where parallel registers were kept, one recording the same information as before and the other being the new style of printed register.

A single baptism record for an identifiable sibling in one of these more detailed registers can sometimes be the key to establishing earlier ancestry.

Printed baptism registers were introduced in some parishes in 1783 when Stamp Duty was imposed on entries in parish registers. Rose's Act required printed baptism registers to be used in all parishes from 1813. The details to be recorded were the date of baptism, the child's Christian name, both parents' Christian names and surname, their abode, the occupation of the father, and the name of the clergyman performing the ceremony. Each entry in the register was numbered. A typical entry in a post-1813 baptism register appears as:

BAPTISMS solemnized in the Parish of *Wedmore* in the County of *Somerset* in the Year 18*18*						
When Baptized.	Child's Christian Name.	Parents Name.		Abode.	Quality, Trade, or Profession.	By whom the Ceremony was performed.
		Christian.	Surname.			
30th April No. 324	William Son of	John & Jemima	Caple	Houghton	Labourer	W.B. Cattles Curate

A few clergymen recorded more information in the new registers than was required, such as the child's date of birth and the mother's maiden name.

Burial Registers

The preservation of bodies after death was both difficult and expensive. Preserving the body of Admiral Horatio Nelson between his death at the Battle of Trafalgar in October 1805 and burial at St Paul's Cathedral in January 1806 required placing it in a cask filled with brandy. Burials of lesser mortals therefore usually took place within a week, and often within three days. Men who died on board ship were usually buried at sea. Unlike a date of baptism, which can sometimes be much later than a date of birth, a date of burial is almost always a reliable approximation of a date of death.

As was the case with baptism registers, the amount of information in burial registers before 1813 was very variable. Sometimes only the date of burial and the name of the deceased person were recorded, for example:

26 April 1766   Joseph Semple

Such a record could relate to a person of any age, ranging from infancy to extreme old age. The Christian names of married women and widows were sometimes omitted, with names recorded as 'Wife of Thomas Bushell' or 'Widow Bushell'.

When only the name was recorded, establishing the identity of the deceased person usually requires corroborating evidence from other sources, such as monumental inscriptions, wills and Poor Law documents, which cannot always be found. However, a significant proportion of burial records contained some genealogical information, such as the name of the father or parents of a deceased child and the name of the husband of a deceased woman. For example:

5 August 1783   Mary the daughter of Thomas and
                     Elizabeth Bushell
8 September 1783   Elizabeth the wife of Thomas Bushell

The amount of information recorded in the burial registers of many parishes increased from the late 1760s onwards, but continued to be minimal in others, with only the name of the deceased person being recorded until the end of 1812. Occupation was never routinely recorded in burial registers, even in the new printed registers introduced in 1813. Before 1813, occupation was recorded in some parishes for periods of time, and sometimes in instances where the deceased person was a temporary resident, such as a soldier or militiaman. More information was usually recorded in the burial registers of those parishes in which more detailed baptism registers were also being kept. These burial registers might include details such as the date of death, the age, the occupation, and genealogical information relating to married women, widows and children. Age at death was recorded in some parishes from the late 1760s and in many parishes in the dioceses of Carlisle and Norwich after 1770. The printed burial registers that were introduced in some parishes after 1783 following the introduction of Stamp Duty made provision for recording the age at death.

As with baptism registers, the burial registers of those parishes that adopted the Dade system included much more information than was generally recorded elsewhere. This included 'Descent, Profession, and Abode', the date of death, the age, and often the cause of death. Some burial records for children recorded the names of both sets of grandparents and their abodes. Burial registers in the Diocese of Durham in the Barrington period from 1798 to 1812 recorded the date of death, the abode, the age, and a variety of other genealogical information. A typical burial record of a widow at Whickham in Co. Durham includes her maiden name, deceased husband's name and his occupation:

> Eleanor Emerson, late Manners, of Fellside, died 27 November, buried 2 December 1810, age: 80, widow of John Emerson, wagonman

Cause of death was routinely recorded in the burial registers of some parishes in the dioceses of York and Durham during the Dade and Barrington periods, but in only a very small number of parishes elsewhere, such as St Philip and St Jacob in Bristol, where both age and cause of death were recorded from 1781 to 1812. Cause of death was sometimes recorded elsewhere when it was the result of an accident, such as drowning, or a contagious disease. Epidemics of diseases such as measles and smallpox were often the cause of multiple deaths in the same family within days, could result in a sharp increase in the number of recorded burials. A few clergymen were in the habit of recording deaths that had taken place in unusual circumstances in some detail.

The details to be recorded in the printed registers introduced in 1813 as a result of George Rose's Act were the name of the deceased, the abode, the date of burial, the age and the name of the clergyman performing the ceremony:

BURIALS in the Parish of *Frome Selwood* in the county of *Somerset* in the Year 1823				
Name.	Abode.	When buried.	Age.	By whom the Ceremony was performed.
Mary King No. 1983.	*Lower Keyford*	*July 27th*	*44*	*J. Harward*

There was no provision for recording the names of the parents of a deceased child, or the husband of a deceased woman, although a few clergymen did record such information. Unlike the baptism registers introduced in 1813, which recorded the occupation of the father, there was no provision for recording occupation in the new burial registers.

Marriage Registers

There is a significant difference between the amount of information recorded in the marriage registers of the Georgian era and those introduced in 1837. Marriage registers before 1837 did not routinely record the names of the fathers of the bride and groom, and there was no requirement to record the ages of the parties or the groom's occupation. The marriage registers of the Georgian era can be divided into two groups, corresponding to the periods before and after 1754, when Hardwicke's Marriage Act came into effect.

Various aspects of English marriage law relevant to genealogical research have been clarified in recent years by Rebecca Probert, a leading academic authority in this area (Probert, 2016). She presents convincing evidence that the assertion in many older books that so-called 'common law' marriages were both widespread and legally valid before 1754 is a myth. Before 1754, marriage was governed by Anglican canon law rather than by statute. The one legal requirement for a marriage to be valid was that it had to be performed by an ordained Anglican clergyman. Canon law required that a marriage should be preceded by the calling of banns or the issuing of a licence and celebrated in the church of the parish in which one of the parties was resident. However, a marriage performed by a clergyman was still legally valid even when neither of these conditions had been fulfilled.

Some marriages before 1754 took place in parishes that were not the normal place of residence of bride or groom, but complied with canon law in all other respects. These are sometimes referred to as *irregular* marriages. Marriage licences could be obtained from the diocesan authorities, and also from certain clergymen known as surrogates. It was possible for a couple to travel to a town or city where marriage licences could be obtained (generally within twenty miles of their home parish but occasionally further afield) and to get married there, usually on the day after the licence was issued. Certain churches in towns and cities became popular venues, as did cathedrals. Because marriage by licence was more expensive than after banns, most couples who married in this way were from slightly more prosperous backgrounds. Some marriages may have taken place in parishes away from the home area for reasons of privacy, or because other family members lived there. However, the reason some couples from rural areas married in local market towns before 1754 may simply have been to have a 'day out'.

Marriages performed by clergymen, but without banns or licence and usually not in a church building, were known as *clandestine* marriages. Most clandestine marriages took place in London, where the most popular venue was the vicinity of the Fleet Prison, a debtors' prison situated in the parish of St Bride Fleet Street. In the late seventeenth century its chapel, together with taverns and houses in the surrounding area, began to be used for secret marriages, and subsequently for marriages taking place openly between couples who wished to marry quickly and at minimal cost. These ceremonies were performed by imprisoned but ordained clergymen. The number of clandestine marriages increased dramatically in the early eighteenth century. By the 1740s over half the marriages in London, although not necessarily of Londoners, and one-seventh of all marriages in England, were taking place in the vicinity of the Fleet Prison. Clandestine marriages also took place at other locations in London, such as the vicinity of the King's Bench Prison and Mayfair Chapel, which was used mainly by the middle and upper classes. Clandestine marriages were recorded in registers to provide a record for legal purposes, but the information recorded is not always reliable, as some registers contain duplicate records and others are known to be forged. Parish of abode was usually recorded. Surviving Fleet marriage records are now held at TNA and have been digitized.

The Fleet Prison in London. Many marriages took place in its vicinity in the first half of the eighteenth century.

In 1754, *An Act for the Better Preventing of Clandestine Marriages*, commonly known as 'Hardwicke's Marriage Act', came into effect. A marriage could now only take place in the parish where one of the parties had been living for at least four weeks and after the calling of banns or the issuing of a licence. The only exception was marriage with a special licence from the Faculty Office of the Archbishop of Canterbury. Such licences permitted marriages to take place anywhere, but they were expensive and only issued in exceptional circumstances. Marriages in locations such as the Fleet Prison came to an end when Hardwicke's Act came into effect, and many London parishes subsequently experienced a significant increase. Numbers fell in churches throughout the country which had become popular venues for people in the surrounding areas. No further marriage ceremonies were performed in most cathedrals and the numbers dropped considerably in others. For example, no further marriages took place at Chester cathedral because its precincts were extra-parochial. Marriages only took place at Exeter Cathedral, which was also the parish church of the Precinct of the Cathedral Close, when one or both parties lived in the parish.

One option after 1754 for people in England who did not wish to marry in their local parish church was to marry in Scotland, where Hardwicke's Act did not apply. Marriage in Scotland could take place by declaration before witnesses and did not require parental consent for the marriage of minors. Several 'marriage houses' were established on the Scottish border, and became popular with English couples, particularly Nonconformists, living within travelling distance, and also with runaway couples from all parts of England. The most famous of these marriage venues was Gretna Green, but there were several others along the border between England and Scotland from west to east. Some records of these 'irregular Border marriages' have survived, and further information is available on the National Records of Scotland website.

Before 1754, the information recorded in marriage registers varied, and was usually minimal, often comprising only the names of the bride and groom, for example:

7 September 1738   Anthony Coles and Mary Billington

Other information that was sometimes recorded included parish of residence of the bride and groom, whether one or both parties was a widow or widower, and whether the marriage had taken place after banns or by licence.

Hardwicke's Act stipulated that a record was to be made at the time of the marriage and signed by the bride and groom, two or more witnesses, and the clergyman performing the ceremony. Each marriage record was to conform to specific wording as specified in the Act:

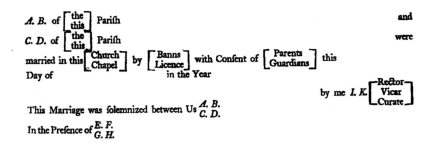

Witnesses could be relatives, friends or church officials. Examination of several pages of a marriage register can often enable the names of regular witnesses to be identified, usually the Parish Clerk or a Churchwarden, and the possibility that they might have been relatives eliminated.

Hardwicke's Marriage Act required the calling of banns and solemnization of marriages to be recorded in registers with numbered pages. Although printed volumes were subsequently used in the majority of parishes, this was not a requirement of the Act. All the marriage records in some parishes, containing a great deal of repetitive wording, were written out by hand. Many different printers sold marriage and banns registers, of which there were two main types. In the first type banns and marriages were recorded separately, either in separate registers or in separate sections of the same volume.

The second type was a composite register in which each entry consisted of two parts: the first part recorded the calling of banns and the second part recorded the solemnization of the marriage.

Both parts were completed when a marriage took place in the same parish as banns had been called. Only the first part was completed when banns were called in two parishes and the marriage took place in the other parish. Only the second part was completed when a marriage took place by licence. In the majority of cases both parts were completed, as it was more common for banns to be called in only one parish, and in most parishes many more marriages took place after banns than by licence.

Marriages between couples from different parishes traditionally took place in the bride's parish, but they sometimes took place in the groom's. Although required by Hardwicke's Act, the consent of parents or guardians was not always recorded in marriage registers before 1813, as most printed registers did not include a specific section for recording it.

Additional information, not specified in Hardwicke's Act, was recorded in the marriage registers of some parishes, particularly the groom's occupation. The ages of the bride and groom, and sometimes their fathers' names, were recorded in the marriage registers of some parishes in the Diocese of York that had adopted the Dade system for baptisms and burials, but such information was rarely recorded elsewhere.

The implementation of George Rose's Act in 1813 had little effect on the contents of marriage registers, but new and standardized printed registers were introduced, with banns now recorded in separate volumes. The new marriage registers specifically included a section 'With consent of _____', for recording the consent of parents or guardians. Although people under the age of 21 needed the consent of their parents to marry, if parents had not opposed the calling of banns they were deemed to have consented.

The inclusion of any further description of the bride and groom, such as 'bachelor', 'spinster', 'widow', 'widower', 'minor', 'bachelor and a minor' or 'spinster and a minor', was not specified in Hardwicke's Act, but most printed registers introduced in 1754 provided a space for such information to be recorded and some provided examples of completed entries in which such information was included. Although the recording of marital status after 1754 was more common than previously, this important information was not always recorded. For example, marital status is routinely absent from the marriage registers of most Westminster parishes between 1754 and 1837. The possible omission of the marital status of a woman marrying as a widow presents a particular challenge to researchers before 1837, as it can result in the identification of an incorrect baptism record. Marital status was generally included in marriage licence records and sometimes in banns registers, but otherwise identifying a woman marrying as a widow but not recorded as such may be dependent on investigating the wider family and finding clues in other sources.

Divorce was to all intents and purposes non-existent during the Georgian era, as it required a private Act of Parliament.

Banns Registers

Few records relating to the calling of banns before 1754 have survived, but Hardwicke's Act required this information to be recorded in registers. When marriage was not by licence, the Act required banns to be called on three successive Sundays in the parishes of both bride and groom, after which the marriage could take place in either parish. Although composite registers containing records of both banns and marriages have usually survived, there was no requirement for registers containing only banns to be kept, so their survival is more variable.

When a bride and groom were living in different parishes in populous areas, banns may only have been called in one, with both parties claiming to be 'of this parish', as having banns called in only one parish was cheaper than having them called in both. There is also evidence that marriages took place in towns and cities between couples from the surrounding area who both claimed to be 'of this parish' but did not actually live there, although in some cases the bride might have been employed in the parish as a domestic servant before the marriage. Such deception is likely to have been easy to get away with in populous parishes, and some clergymen may have turned a blind eye.

The marital status of the bride and groom was sometimes recorded in banns registers when not recorded in marriage registers. When banns were called in two parishes, the marital status of the bride or groom as a widow or a widower may only have been recorded in the banns register of the parish in which the marriage did not take place.

A record of the calling of banns is not necessarily an indication that the marriage actually took place. The parents of a minor could forbid a marriage by opposing the banns and such opposition was sometimes recorded in banns registers. Some couples or one of the parties may have changed their minds at the last minute. A variety of unforeseen circumstances may have prevented marriages from taking place after banns had been called, such as sudden illness or death, imprisonment for crime or debt, or impressment into the navy during wartime. Some banns records have crept into marriage indexes when there is no evidence that marriages ever took place. It is therefore very important always to check original records and not to rely only on indexes.

OTHER PARISH RECORDS

A variety of other ecclesiastical records were kept by parishes, of varying degrees of relevance to family history research, but their survival is very variable. Most parish records of the Georgian era have been deposited in archives, where they are available either in their original format or as microfilm copies, but relatively few have been digitized. Although they can sometimes be rich sources of family history information, few records, apart from local census listings, have been indexed by name. Searching for information relating to individuals usually involves browsing through the records page by page, with no guarantee that anything will be found. Records for some parishes have been transcribed by volunteers, often local history researchers. Older transcripts are sometimes held in archives and local studies libraries and some have been published. More recent transcripts may be available online, sometimes on local history or parish websites. The main categories of parish records other than parish registers of potential relevance to family history researchers are discussed below. Further information can be found in Tate (1969), Raymond (2015) and Raymond (2017b).

Records of the Vestry, Churchwardens and Overseers

As mentioned in the previous chapter, each parish was governed by a Vestry, which consisted of the clergyman and a number of ratepayers. There were two types of Vestry meeting. Open Vestries included all the ratepayers. Closed or Select Vestries were restricted to the clergyman, Churchwardens and a select number of principal inhabitants. Some Select Vestries were selected by Open Vestries, whereas others were self-perpetuating oligarchies. Vestries with twenty-four members were often referred to as the 'four and twenty'. The content of Vestry minutes varies considerably from parish to parish. Many Vestry minutes recorded only administrative matters such as the appointment of parish officers and the setting of rates, but some recorded information about parishioners, such as children bound as parish apprentices. The Select Vestries set up from 1819 under the Sturges Bourne Act, with specific responsibility for Poor Law matters, are discussed with other aspects of the Poor Law in Chapter 9.

Parish officers were appointed by the Vestry from the parish ratepayers on an annual basis. Rates were paid only by more prosperous inhabitants, and were based on the value of the land they owned or occupied. The parish officers in rural areas therefore usually included farmers but not agricultural labourers. Parish officers could usually read and write, or at the very least sign their names, so their signatures in parish records may be useful for identification purposes.

Churchwardens were the senior parish officers and had both ecclesiastical and civil duties, including responsibility for the administration of the Poor Law, but in most parishes this responsibility was delegated to separate Overseers of the Poor. Most parishes had two Churchwardens, often with one elected by the ratepayers (the *people's warden*) and the other chosen by the clergyman (the *vicar's warden*). Churchwardens collected church rates for the upkeep of the church and Overseers collected poor rates for the maintenance of the poor.

Parish officers employed a range of tradesmen in the maintenance of the church building and any poor house that had been established in the parish, and in providing poor relief to paupers. The amount of detail recorded in the accounts kept by Churchwardens and Overseers varied considerably, but they often included the names and occupations of tradesmen and the goods and services they provided. Occupations regularly appearing in Churchwardens' and Overseers' accounts include carpenters, stonemasons, blacksmiths, tailors, shoemakers, butchers, bakers, clock-winders and rat-catchers. The trades involved were often passed from father to son, so the information recorded can sometimes provide clues to genealogical relationships.

Tithe Records

Parish incumbents received an income from tithes, which were taxes on agricultural produce. Payments of tithes in kind were gradually replaced by monetary payments. Annual payments based on land value were introduced following the Tithes Commutation Act of 1836. A land survey took place, which resulted in the production of *tithe maps and apportionments*. As they were produced after the Georgian era had ended they are not discussed in this book, but further information can be found in Kain and Prince (2000). Tithes were often extinguished in exchange for land by parliamentary enclosure, which was at its height in the period from 1760 to 1830, and is discussed in Chapter 10.

Whether a parish had a rector, a vicar or a perpetual curate was dependent on how tithes had been apportioned at the time of the dissolution of the monasteries under Henry VIII. Tithes were divided into greater or rectorial tithes, levied on wheat, hay and wood, and lesser or vicarial tithes, levied on all other produce. A rector was entitled to the greater and lesser tithes, a vicar to the lesser tithes only and a perpetual curate received no tithes. Each parish with a vicar had a lay rector, known as an impropriator, entitled to collect the greater tithes, and usually also being the patron with the right to appoint the vicar. The impropriator could be an individual or an institution, such as an Oxford or Cambridge college. The clergyman of a parochial chapelry, or a parish that had been created out of one, was usually a perpetual curate, with all tithes being paid to the rector or vicar of the ancient parish of which the chapelry was or had once been a part.

Tithe account books relating to the Georgian era have survived for some parishes. Annual listings of people who paid tithes can be useful in the absence of other sources listing owners and occupiers of land, such as lists of ratepayers and Land Tax records. Disputes over tithes were very common, and sometimes involved litigation in the ecclesiastical, common law and equity courts. The records of many tithe disputes have survived both in parish records and the papers of landowning families, and can often be identified by searching archive catalogues. Such records may include a great deal of information about more prosperous parish inhabitants and the land they owned.

Records of Pew Rents

The seating arrangement in churches reflected the social hierarchy of the period, with more prosperous inhabitants occupying private pews towards the front of the church and poorer inhabitants sitting on benches at the back, or standing in populous parishes. Private pews were rented, and often remained in the same family for many generations. Records relating to seating allocation and payment of pew rents have sometimes survived in parish records.

Local Censuses and Parochial Surveys

Detailed lists of inhabitants were made in some parishes in connection with the decennial censuses from 1801 to 1831. Although there was no requirement for lists to be kept, they have survived for a few parishes, usually in parish records. Various listings of parish inhabitants were made throughout the Georgian era on the initiative of individual clergymen. They often recorded religious affiliation, and sometimes the number of bibles and prayer books in each household. Some of these listings contain more information about household members than was recorded in later censuses, although they rarely record place of birth. Such listings are relatively rare, but because they are such a valuable source of information, they have often been transcribed by individuals and family history societies, and some transcriptions are now available online. Further information on pre-1841 census listings can be found in Chapman (2002). Militia ballot lists, listing male parish inhabitants of military age, are described with other militia records in Chapter 7.

Chapter 4

HIGHER ECCLESIASTICAL JURISDICTIONS

Many records were kept by Church of England jurisdictions at a higher level than the parish. The categories of record that are particularly relevant to family history researchers are:

- Wills and other records relating to probate and administration.
- Records relating to the issuing of marriage licences.
- Bishop's transcripts.
- Cause papers and other records relating to cases in the church courts.

These sources, together with the main historical factors that have influenced their current location in archives, are discussed in this chapter.

THE CHURCH OF ENGLAND AND ITS RECORDS

The Church of England was established by Henry VIII in the sixteenth century and its structure remained virtually unchanged until the very end of the Georgian era. Certain functions, such as the proving of wills, were carried out in a range of ecclesiastical courts that reflected the hierarchical structure of the church. As is still the case today, each diocese, headed by a bishop, lay in one of the two provinces (or archbishoprics) of Canterbury and York. Each diocese was subdivided into several archdeaconries headed by archdeacons. There was no direct relationship between ecclesiastical boundaries and county boundaries, but many archdeaconries covered substantially the same areas as counties, so most counties lay within a single diocese. However, Warwickshire was divided between the dioceses of Worcester and Lichfield & Coventry, most of Shropshire between the dioceses of Lichfield & Coventry and Hereford, and the North Riding of Yorkshire between the dioceses of York and Chester. Archdeaconries were subdivided into groups of adjacent parishes called deaneries, sometimes referred to as rural deaneries. The Church of England therefore had the following hierarchical structure:

Province of Canterbury or York
Diocese
Archdeaconry
Deanery
Parish

Deaneries kept few records, but the records of dioceses and archdeaconries were sometimes organized by deanery. In most dioceses, authority to perform certain functions, such as proving wills, was delegated to some or all archdeaconries, but in others this authority remained centralized. The history, structure and records of the Church of England are described in Raymond (2017b).

Dioceses were the most significant organizational unit of the Church of England above parishes. Their boundaries remained static for most of the Georgian era, but many changes have taken place since 1836. The forty dioceses of today include the original twenty-two post-Reformation English dioceses (Bath & Wells, Bristol, Canterbury, Carlisle, Chester, Chichester, Durham, Ely, Exeter, Gloucester, Hereford, Lichfield & Coventry, Lincoln, London, Norwich, Oxford, Peterborough, Rochester, Salisbury, Winchester, Worcester and York), but their boundaries have changed and the majority are now much smaller.

Records relating to parish inhabitants could potentially have been in the custody of parishes, peculiar jurisdictions, archdeaconries, dioceses, and the provinces of Canterbury and York. Most of these records have now been deposited in archives, but the records relevant to a single parish and its inhabitants are not necessarily all held in the

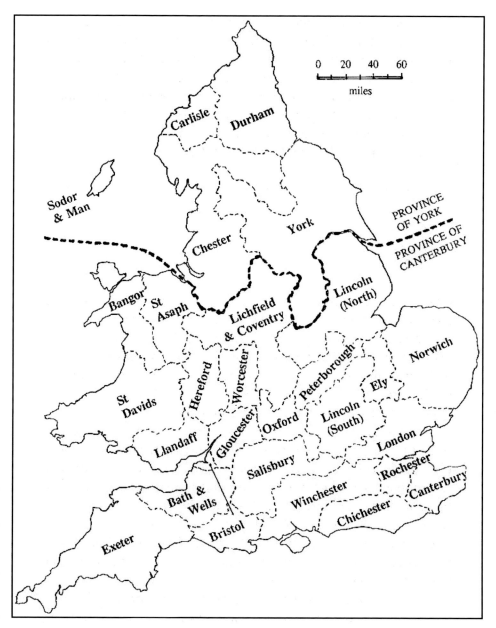

The dioceses of England and Wales before 1835 (reproduced with permission from Sin, Sex and Probate *by Colin R. Chapman, Lochin Publishing, p.36.)*

same one. The location of records is relevant not only when visiting archives in person but also to accessing resources online. Different types of record relating to the same parish, but held in different archives, may be available through different online search services. There may also be a significant disparity in the extent to which the holdings of different archives are available online at all.

The current location of records originally held at archdeaconry or diocesan level is dependent on the boundaries that existed during the Georgian era. The maps from *The Phillimore Atlas and Index of Parish Registers*, edited by Cecil Humphery-Smith (2003), mentioned in the previous chapter, show the boundaries of dioceses, archdeaconries and peculiars that existed in 1832. Records originally held by archdeaconries, most of whose boundaries were similar to those of counties, are often held in the relevant county archive (record office). However, different categories of record may be held in different archives. For example, church court and marriage licence records for the Archdeaconry of Nottingham are held at the University of Nottingham's Manuscripts and Special Collections, while probate records and bishop's transcripts are held at Nottinghamshire Archives.

Most of the records of the dioceses that existed during the Georgian era are now held by the archives that hold the parish records for the present-day dioceses of the same name, but some are held in a different archive in the same area.

Most records originally held by the Province of Canterbury are now held at Lambeth Palace Library in London, but the probate records of the Prerogative Court of Canterbury are held at TNA. Records of the Province of York are held at the Borthwick Institute in York.

Records of peculiars are not necessarily held in the archives holding records of the dioceses within which they were geographically situated. For example, several parishes in south-west Northumberland lay within the peculiar of Hexhamshire of the Archbishop of York, so records are held at the Borthwick Institute in York.

The use of maps, printed guides and relevant websites is therefore essential to establish the current location of records produced by higher ecclesiastical jurisdictions, whether attempting to access them

Lincoln Cathedral. The Diocese of Lincoln was the largest diocese in England during the Middle Ages, stretching from the Thames to the Humber. During the Georgian era it was still much larger than it is today, and was divided into two disconnected parts, separated by the Diocese of Peterborough.

in archives or online. As well as the maps in the Phillimore Atlas, which shows ecclesiastical boundaries, information on the current location of probate records, marriage licence records and bishop's transcripts can be found in two pamphlets published by The Family History Partnership, referred to in the relevant sections below. More detailed local information can be found in books on researching ancestors in specific areas and the websites of local archives and family history societies. The FamilySearch Wiki indicates the ecclesiastical jurisdictions for individual parishes, and detailed information for some counties can be found on the GENUKI website.

Knowledge of changes in county and diocesan boundaries and the custodial history of records can often explain why Church of England records are now held in locations that can appear arbitrary or illogical. This is particularly relevant in counties such as Yorkshire, where many changes in county and diocesan boundaries have taken place since the Georgian era. In the previous chapter it was mentioned that parish records for certain parishes in Teesdale, such as Romaldkirk and Bowes, which were in the North Riding of Yorkshire before 1974, but are now in Co. Durham, are held at Durham County Record Office. Before 1836, when the new Diocese of Ripon was created, parishes in this part of the North Riding lay within the large Archdeaconry of Richmond of the Diocese of Chester, which was subdivided into Western Deaneries in Lancashire and Eastern Deaneries in Yorkshire. Archdeaconry records relating to the Eastern Deaneries are now held by West Yorkshire Archive Service in Leeds. Probate records, marriage licence documents and bishop's transcripts relating to the western half of the North Riding of Yorkshire are therefore now held in a different archive to those of its eastern half, which are held at the Borthwick Institute in York.

Probate Records

Wills are an extremely valuable source of information for family history researchers, as not only do they contain information about genealogical relationships, but they can also tell us a great deal about ancestors' lives. It has been estimated that 6–10 per cent of the population made wills. Many people only made wills when they believed they were close to death, so sudden death may have prevented some people from making wills who might otherwise have done so.

A will had to be proved to enable the executors to assume control of the deceased person's estate, but it is likely that the estates of some testators were distributed informally without probate, so their wills are unlikely to have survived. Wills that reached the probate courts were made by people from all levels of society, but the probability of finding a will increases with the prosperity of the individual. It is fairly common to find wills for surgeons and lawyers but rare to find any for agricultural labourers. Most wills were proved within a few months of the testator's death, but a small minority were not proved until several decades afterwards.

The ownership of a woman's property automatically passed to her husband on marriage. Married women could make wills in certain circumstances, but relatively few did so, and most wills were made by men, widows and unmarried women. Some wills consisted of many pages, containing a great deal of complex legal verbiage, but others of only a few lines. The amount of information they contain relating to relationships between individuals is very variable, and the length of wills does not necessarily reflect their genealogical content.

The main genealogical value of wills, particularly before civil registration, lies in their potential to explain or confirm relationships between individuals not recorded in other sources. For example, suppose that the marriage of Thomas Acheson and Mary Teasdale has been found in 1802, but the identity of Mary's father is unknown or uncertain, because marriage records before 1837 did not record this information and either no baptism can be found or there are several possible baptisms for people with the same name in the same area around the estimated year of birth. If Mary's father, William Teasdale, had made a will in which he referred to 'my daughter Mary the wife of Thomas Acheson', this would confirm that Mary was the daughter of William Teasdale.

Wills of elderly testators, particularly when they included the full names of married daughters and sometimes married granddaughters, are particularly valuable in supplementing the often minimal information in parish registers. Some of the most genealogically valuable wills are those of elderly bachelors, spinsters, and childless widows and widowers, who often mentioned a wide range of family members, including brothers, sisters, nephews, nieces, great-nephews and great-nieces, sometimes enabling a complex family tree of two or three generations to be constructed from the contents of a single will. Wills of the siblings of direct ancestors can sometimes enable challenging brick walls to be overcome. Testators who died relatively young sometimes named one or both parents, and the names of parents and grandparents occasionally appear in wills when testators referred to property or heirlooms they had inherited.

Two copies of each will have often survived in the records of probate courts: original wills and registered copies. Original wills were written out by a variety of different people, including testators themselves, lawyers and clergymen, so the handwriting can be very variable, but they include the signatures or marks of the testator and witnesses. The granting of probate, in Latin before 1733, was recorded either by annotating the will, or in a separate document indicating when, where and to whom probate had been granted. Wills are sometimes accompanied by probate bonds, by means of which the executor(s) and sometimes others were legally bound to prove the will or otherwise pay a penal sum. Bonds usually consisted of standard printed forms in which relevant information was inserted, and contain the signatures or marks of the individuals bound.

Registered copies of wills are transcripts of the original wills copied into registers by probate court clerks. They may also include details of when and to whom probate was granted. Unlike original wills, the handwriting is usually fairly uniform, but as with any copy of an earlier source there is a possibility that minor copying errors might have been made.

When a person died intestate (without making a will), but had owned property of significant value, one or more people with an interest in their estate would apply for letters of administration, often referred to simply as an administration, and abbreviated to *Admon*. Administrators were usually close relatives, but sometimes the deceased person's principal creditor. Surviving records of administrations are often in the form of administration bonds, similar to probate bonds.

The amount of genealogical information recorded in administration records varies, but it is often limited to the names of the administrators and their relationship to the deceased person. A small proportion of administrations contain more genealogical information, such as the names of all surviving children under the age of 21.

If a person left a will but did not name executors, or the executor(s) appointed had died or did not wish to act, the probate court would appoint administrators, who were legally bound to execute the will by means of an administration bond. The two documents were kept together as a composite record referred to as *Administration with Will Annexed*.

Brief records of grants of probate and administration were often made in *Act Books*. Act Books are the only surviving record of administrations granted by some probate courts.

Before 1782, the production of an *inventory* of a deceased person's possessions was a legal requirement, but they were only produced after that date when requested by an interested party. Inventories, when they survive, can provide a unique glimpse into aspects of ancestors' lives that can rarely be obtained from other sources. An inventory for a yeoman, for example, might list the contents of the farmhouse where he had lived room by room. Inventories are sometimes kept with the associated wills or administrations and sometimes as a separate collection of records.

When a deceased person left children under the age of 21, the guardians appointed were often legally bound to their responsibilities by means of *tuition bonds* or *curation bonds*, which are usually held with wills and administrations.

Before 1858 there were 372 probate courts of various sizes. The larger probate courts reflected the hierarchical structure of the Church of England, and included the prerogative courts of York and Canterbury, consistory (diocesan) courts and archdeaconry courts. There were also 285 peculiar courts of many different types.

Wills of people living in the same parish in Georgian England can potentially be found in the records of several probate jurisdictions. The probate court at which a will was proved was dependent on where the testator held personal property, and not on the place of death or the normal place of abode. Property was only of significance for probate purposes when over a certain value, known as *bona notabilia* (notable goods). This was generally defined as goods valued at over £5, or £10 in London.

If a testator held *bona notabilia* in only one archdeaconry, the will would normally be proved at the archdeaconry court, if one existed. Jurisdiction over probate matters was delegated to all archdeaconries in most dioceses, selectively in some, and not at all in others. For example, the Archdeaconry of Nottingham, corresponding to the county of Nottinghamshire, was the only one of the four archdeaconries of the Diocese of York to have its own probate court. None of the archdeaconries within the Diocese of Lichfield & Coventry had jurisdiction over probate matters. Wills of people living in Derbyshire, and having *bona notabilia* only within the Archdeaconry of Derby, were proved at the consistory court.

If a testator held *bona notabilia* in more than one archdeaconry within the same diocese, the will would normally be proved at the consistory court. If a testator held *bona notabilia* in more than one diocese, the will would be proved at the Prerogative Court of York (PCY) or Prerogative Court of Canterbury (PCC), as appropriate. If a testator held *bona notabilia* in both provinces, the will would be proved in both prerogative courts, but with the grant of probate limited to property held in that particular province.

The majority of testators held property in only one place, so most wills were proved in the lowest applicable court. However, probate could be obtained in any higher court having jurisdiction over the area concerned. Obtaining probate in higher courts than was strictly necessary became more common in the early nineteenth century, and many more wills were proved at the PCC. The PCC, which was actually in London, had jurisdiction over probate matters in the whole of England and Wales, so the wills of testators who held *bona notabilia* only within the province of York could be proved at the PCC, but not the other way around. During the eighteenth century the majority of wills proved at the PCC were for fairly wealthy individuals, but in the early nineteenth century an increasing number were for people from lower down the social scale whose wills would previously have been proved in lower courts.

The wills of people who died overseas, including soldiers and sailors, were also proved at the PCC. Researchers whose lower-class ancestors lived in the north of England should therefore not entirely ignore PCC probate records, as they can potentially include wills or administrations for family members who died while serving in the army or navy.

The registered copies of PCC wills, written in a distinctive script, are held at TNA. They have been digitized and are available online through several different online search services. Original wills have not been digitized, so looking at them requires either visiting TNA or ordering copies. PCC administrations have not yet been digitized and most cannot be searched online, although an online index to those from 1750–1800 is available to members of the Society of Genealogists. Otherwise, searching PCC administrations requires using a combination of typescript and manuscript indexes on the premises at TNA. The most detailed guide to PCC records that has been published is Scott (1997).

The probate records of the PCY can be searched on Findmypast and copies can be ordered from the Borthwick Institute in York.

Many indexes of wills proved in diocesan, archdeaconry and peculiar courts have been published, and many indexes are now available online. Wills are also included in the online catalogues of some archives. Some probate records have been digitized by Ancestry, Findmypast and FamilySearch. Examples of digitized probate collections include those for the Archdeaconry of Dorset (covering most of Dorset but excluding some peculiars) available on Ancestry, and those for the Diocese of Lichfield & Coventry (covering Staffordshire, Derbyshire, and parts of Warwickshire and Shropshire) on Findmypast. The probate records for some counties, such as Durham, Northumberland, Cheshire and Kent, have been digitized by FamilySearch and the images are freely available and browseable, but not all are searchable via the FamilySearch website. Probate records held at Essex Record Office (covering Essex and eastern Hertfordshire) can be identified by searching the online archive catalogue, but accessing the images requires paying a subscription or visiting the archive premises. The only search tools for some probate collections, however, are card indexes at archive premises.

It is advisable to search the records of all the courts that had jurisdiction over the area concerned, although it may be found that some higher courts were either used very little or not at all. For example, because of its distance, the Consistory Court of Chester was bypassed for proving the wills of testators in the western half of the North Riding of Yorkshire that lay within the Archdeaconry of Richmond. Most of these wills were proved at the Archdeaconry court, some at the PCY, and a small proportion at the PCC.

When probate became a civil responsibility in 1858 the records of most probate courts were transferred to the new regional probate registries, where they remained until after the Second World War. They were subsequently transferred to local archives in the 1950s and 1960s. In 1942 the Exeter Probate Registry was destroyed in an air raid. The records that were lost include all probate records for the archdeaconry, diocesan and peculiar courts of the Dioceses of Exeter and Bath & Wells, mainly relating to testators from Devon and Somerset. Some probate records of testators from Cornwall, proved in the diocesan and peculiar courts, were also lost, but the majority survived, as they had been proved at the court of the Archdeaconry of Cornwall. These wills were held at the Bodmin Probate Registry in 1942.

Death Duty (sometimes referred to as Estate Duty) registers were kept by the Board of Stamps (later the Inland Revenue) from 1796, and are now held at TNA in series IR 26. The proportion of estates of sufficient value to be subject to Death Duty gradually increased, and after 1815 most wills and administrations are included in these registers. Death Duty registers sometimes contain a great deal of information about testators and their families. The indexes to the Death Duty registers, in series IR 27, which are available on Findmypast, are a valuable resource in themselves, as they can enable most wills and administrations in the full range of English probate courts in the early nineteenth century to be identified. Each index entry includes the name of the executor or administrator and their place of abode, together with the name of the court in which probate or administration was granted. These indexes can therefore enable wills and administrations in collections not currently searchable online to be identified. The inclusion of information about executors and administrators can also enable wills and administrations for other family members to be identified relatively easily.

The Death Duty registers themselves, which are only partially available online, often contain information about beneficiaries not included in wills, such as addresses, names of children (information that can be particularly helpful when a testator referred to 'my children' without naming them), and dates of birth and death. Death Duty registers can also provide relevant genealogical information when people died intestate and only minimal details are available from administration records. Surviving country court (i.e. excluding the PCC) Death Duty registers from 1796 to 1811 have been digitized, and records for individuals can be identified using TNA's Discovery catalogue. Accessing the registers from 1812 onwards currently requires either visiting TNA, where they are available on microfilm, or at a LDS family history centre, where digital images can be accessed through FamilySearch.

From 1812, copies of wills were required to be sent to the Board of Stamps in London, but the copies relating to most probate jurisdictions were intentionally destroyed in the 1960s, as they duplicated existing records. Copies of wills proved in probate courts in the south west of England whose records had been lost in 1942 were extracted from this collection before its destruction and sent to the relevant county record offices to act as substitutes for the lost wills.

Further information on probate records can be found in Grannum and Taylor (2009) and Raymond (2012b). Their locations and availability online are listed by county in Gibson and Raymond (2016).

Marriage Licence Records

Marriages could take place after the calling of banns or by presenting the clergyman with a marriage licence. Marriages by licence could take place more quickly and with less publicity, but were more expensive. The people who married by licence were usually from more prosperous backgrounds, but also included many soldiers and sailors.

The majority of marriage licences were issued under the authority of the bishop of the diocese in which the bride and groom were living, but some were issued by the Faculty Office or Vicar General of the Archbishop of Canterbury. In theory, a Faculty Office licence was required when the two parties lived in different provinces and a Vicar General licence when they lived in different dioceses within the province of Canterbury. In practice many couples from more prosperous backgrounds living in the south-east of England married with these licences when it was not strictly necessary. Some marriage licences were issued by designated parish clergymen known as *surrogates*, and some peculiars issued their own marriage licences.

The marriage licence itself was issued to the groom for presentation to the clergyman performing the ceremony, so relatively few have survived, although they are occasionally found in parish records. The surviving documents relating to the issue of marriage licences are the bonds and allegations completed during the application process. The applicant, usually the groom, paid the relevant fee and signed an allegation and a bond. The allegation was a document in which the couple, or often just the groom, alleged that there was no impediment to the marriage. Information about the bride and groom, such as their ages, marital status and place of abode, and sometimes the groom's occupation, was recorded. Ages were often only approximate, with the practice varying from one diocese to another. People aged 21 or over, and able to marry without permission, were often recorded as '21 years of age and upwards', but exact ages were sometimes recorded. Ages were recorded in bands in some dioceses, so a bride or groom aged 37 might be described as '30 years of age and upwards'. The status of minors was recorded, and often their exact age, together with the name of the person giving consent to the marriage, usually the father, or the mother or a guardian if the father was no longer living. The bond was a pledge to pay a penal sum if the allegation proved to be untrue. Marriage bonds were signed by the groom and another person, referred to as the *bondsman*, who was often a close relative of the bride or groom. Marriage bonds repeat some of the details in allegations, but may include further information. Sometimes only one of the two documents has survived.

As an example of the information found in allegations and bonds, an allegation in the Diocese of Bath & Wells dated 27 May 1801 stated that John Knight of Charlton Adam in Somerset was aged 21 years and upwards, and intended to marry Susanna Grabham of Bridgwater, a spinster of the age of 18 years and upwards, and that her father, Thomas Grabham, consented to the marriage. The associated bond with the same date, in which Thomas Grabham was the bondsman, repeated some of this information, and also referred to John Knight as a bachelor and Thomas Grabham as a yeoman. Both documents were signed by John Knight and Thomas Grabham. The marriage took place at Bridgwater the day after the licence was issued.

Marriage licence records can sometimes enable a woman's maiden name to be established when no other records of the marriage can be found. The record of the issue of a marriage licence does not imply that a marriage actually took place, but when subsequent baptisms can be found it is almost certain that it did. The relevant marriage register may not have survived or the marriage may not have been recorded, particularly before 1754 when there was no requirement for registers to be signed after the ceremony.

The issue of marriage licences was generally recorded in Act Books. The information recorded was usually the date of issue of the licence, the names of the parties, and their parishes. Act Books may enable some marriages to be identified when no bonds or allegations have survived. Some Act Books have been indexed but few are searchable online. It is usually feasible to browse through unindexed Act Books for the years during which an elusive marriage is most likely to have taken place, even when no indexes are available.

For a relatively short period from September 1822 to March 1823, copies of the baptism records for both the bride and groom were required to be submitted before a marriage licence was issued. Sworn statements were made when baptism records could not be traced. These records are usually filed with allegations and bonds. The information included, for direct ancestors or identifiable siblings, can be very helpful in tracing the origins of people who had died or left the country before the 1851 census.

The archives in which marriage licence records are held are listed by county in Gibson (2001). Some collections of marriage licence records can be searched online, and a few collections have been digitized. Sometimes the only search tools are typescript or card indexes at archive premises. The marriage licence records in some archives have not been indexed at all, so relevant items can only be identified by browsing through the records chronologically. Faculty Office and Vicar General marriage licence records are held at Lambeth Palace Library and are can be searched on Findmypast. These records are also available on microfilm at the Society of Genealogists, which can supply copies.

Bishop's Transcripts

Transcriptions of the entries in parish registers, known as bishop's transcripts, were required to be made annually and were then stored centrally within dioceses or archdeaconries. Bishop's transcripts were written on separate sheets of paper or parchment, and their survival by diocese varies considerably. For example, bishop's transcripts for the dioceses of Exeter and Bath & Wells are very incomplete for much of the Georgian era, those for the Diocese of Durham only survive from the 1760s, and very few survive for the Diocese of London before 1800. In contrast, the collection of bishop's transcripts for the Diocese of Canterbury is the most complete in England, and there is also a duplicate set of archdeacon's transcripts.

Bishop's transcripts are a particularly valuable resource for periods when original parish registers no longer survive, or if relevant pages are missing, damaged or illegible. Many bishop's transcripts are likely to have been copied directly from parish registers, with the possibility that errors or omissions could have been made. Some bishop's transcripts include more information than the corresponding parish registers, so must have been copied from a different or earlier source, such as a rough notebook. It is therefore quite common to find variations in the content of entries for the same event in the two categories of record. The additional or variant information in bishop's transcripts, particularly in baptism and burial records, can sometimes enable events to be associated with specific individuals when parish registers entries are very brief, and in some cases to enable brick walls to be overcome. For example, the burial register of Cadeleigh in Devon includes the following details of a child buried on 11 September 1772:

Robert Bradford, a child.

The record in the corresponding bishop's transcript appears as:

Robert son of James and Thomasina Bradford of Cruwys Morchard.

Many printed volumes of transcripts of parish registers have been published since the late nineteenth century, and many typescript and manuscript transcripts have also been produced, which are now available in archives, local studies libraries and at the Society of Genealogists. Some of these transcript volumes are composite sequences of records from parish registers and the corresponding bishop's transcripts, in which any variation or additional information in one or the other has been noted.

Bishop's transcripts are not necessarily held in the same archive as the corresponding parish registers. Their locations are listed by county in Gibson (2001). Even when they are held in the same archive, they may not have been included when collections of parish registers have been indexed or digitized. Some collections of bishop's transcripts have been digitized by FamilySearch and are browseable, but not all are name searchable via the FamilySearch website.

Causes in the Church Courts

Both secular and ecclesiastical courts impinged on the lives of individuals at all levels of society in Georgian England. Church courts were responsible for a range of administrative and judicial functions, not limited to matters of religion. Their most important role from the perspective of present-day family history researchers was the proving of wills, discussed earlier in this chapter. Other functions included licensing people to perform certain duties, such as schoolmasters and midwives. Their judicial role included punishing people for a range of moral offences, such as drunkenness, adultery and fornication, which would now be categorized as sins rather than crimes. They also enabled individuals to pursue legal actions against others, particularly for defamation, and in relation to disputes over tithes and wills. The church courts and their records are described in Chapman (1997) and Tarver (1995).

Cases that came before church courts were referred to as *causes*. Causes relating to illicit sexual activity such as fornication and adultery came before the church courts well into the eighteenth century. People found guilty were required to perform a penance, usually involving facing the congregation clothed in a white sheet on several successive Sundays, sometimes in different churches, and reading a confession. The involvement of the church courts in punishing people for moral offences gradually declined during the Georgian era, but their role in disputes between individuals continued.

The records of the church courts include not only statements made by plaintiffs and defendants, but also those of witnesses. Witnesses could be from all levels of society, and the statements they made included information about themselves, such as their age, abode and occupation. Other information that was sometimes recorded included place of birth, how long they had lived in the parish, and the parishes where they had previously lived. In a cause relating to defamation in the Diocese of York in 1751, for example, a witness who was a neighbour of the plaintiff was described as:

> Juliana the wife of Stephen Gibson of the parish of Saint Peter the Little in the City and Diocese of York waterman aged thirty years or thereabouts.

Like other types of court record, unless a clue can be found in some other source, identifying relevant records is usually dependent on the availability of search tools. Although the records of some courts remain unlisted, others have been listed in detail, as cause papers are of interest to historians. They may be searchable by name using archives' online catalogues, although the catalogue records for some collections include only the names of plaintiffs and defendants and not those of witnesses. Other search tools, such as card indexes, may be available at archive premises. Cause papers for the church courts of the Diocese of York have been digitized and the images can be viewed online on the University of Sheffield's Humanities Research Institute (HRI Digital) website.

Chapter 5

RELIGIOUS DISSENT

Several Protestant Nonconformist denominations were established in the seventeenth century and were allowed certain freedoms under the Toleration Act of 1689, but Roman Catholicism continued to be suppressed for a further century. Over 90 per cent of the population were nominally members of the Church of England until the late eighteenth century, after which the numbers of both Nonconformists and Roman Catholics increased dramatically.

Information relevant to both genealogy and family history can potentially be found in a range of Nonconformist and Roman Catholic records, but their survival is very variable. The historical development of the various denominations during the Georgian era is complex, so it is only possible to provide an outline of the major denominations and their records in this chapter. Although published several decades ago, two of the introductory volumes of the *National Index of Parish Registers* provide a comprehensive introduction to the sources available for researching people who were members of churches outside the Church of England. Steel (1973) describes sources for Nonconformists, and Steel and Samuel (1974) describes sources for Roman Catholics (and Jews). Mullet (1991) describes Nonconformist records before 1830. Two books by Stuart Raymond (2017a and forthcoming) include details of a wide range of sources where information on Nonconformists and Roman Catholics can be found. Several books in the *My Ancestor* series, referred to in the relevant sections below, provide information on researching members of specific denominations.

Information on local Nonconformist and Roman Catholic congregations can often be found on archive websites, and some local family history societies have produced lists. The county volumes of the *National Index of Parish Registers*, published by the Society of Genealogists and available in many libraries, list Nonconformist and Roman Catholic registers.

THE THREE DENOMINATIONS: PRESBYTERIANS, INDEPENDENTS AND BAPTISTS

The various Protestant denominations that developed during the seventeenth century were referred to collectively as Nonconformists or Protestant Dissenters. Some Baptist congregations were established in the early seventeenth century. Many Church of England clergymen who were Puritans were ejected from their livings in 1662 because they refused to comply with the Act of Uniformity, and some set up separate congregations, most of which were either Presbyterian or Independent. Presbyterians wanted to remain within a reformed Church of England, but Independents wanted each congregation to be separate, and later became known as Congregationalists. Close links developed between the different Nonconformist denominations in some areas, particularly between Presbyterians and Independents. Some congregations switched allegiance, and there were also many schisms. Nonconformity was strongest in towns and cities, and in those country areas where congregations had been established in 1662 or earlier. Nonconformist churches often drew in people from much wider areas that parish churches.

Presbyterians and Independents were generally of higher social status than Baptists, and were often from middle-class backgrounds. Some English Presbyterians became Unitarians in the early eighteenth century. Further information on sources for researching English Presbyterians and Unitarians can be found in Ruston (2001), for Independents in Clifford (1997) and for Baptists in Breed (2002).

The number of Nonconformists slowly declined during the early and mid-eighteenth century, but the evangelical revival of the late eighteenth century led to the establishment of new congregations in many areas. New Presbyterian churches, often referred to as Scotch churches, sometimes with ministers who had been ordained in the Church of Scotland, were established in the later Georgian period in areas where significant numbers of people of Scottish descent were living. The Presbyterian Church of England and the Congregational Church in England and Wales amalgamated to form the United Reformed Church (URC) in 1972.

The records of the three denominations relevant to genealogy and family history can be divided into two categories: *registers of births, baptisms and burials*, and *church books* and similar records.

Registers of Births, Baptisms and Burials

Not all Nonconformist churches kept records of births and baptisms. Some registers were kept by individual ministers, who took them with them if they moved away. Baptist congregations did not practise infant baptism, but usually recorded the baptisms of adults and sometimes the births of children. The survival of birth and baptism registers for Nonconformist congregations during the Georgian era is very variable. They survive for the whole period for some congregations, but only from the late eighteenth or early nineteenth centuries for others. The amount of information recorded in baptism registers varies, but the records are often fuller than in standard Church of England baptism registers of the same period. The date of birth was often recorded, and sometimes the mother's maiden name.

Most Nonconformists married in parish churches before 1754, and the law required all Nonconformists apart from Quakers (discussed below) to marry in the Church of England between 1754 and 1837. Some Nonconformist churches established their own burial grounds, but otherwise members of their congregations were buried in their local parish churchyard.

The absence of baptism records for a whole generation of siblings, when relevant marriage and burial records can be found in parish registers, is a strong indication of Nonconformity. When Nonconformist churches had burial grounds, marriages may be found in Anglican marriage registers, but with fewer baptisms and burials for relevant surnames in parish registers than might be expected, or sometimes none at all. Baptisms and burials not recorded in parish registers can often be found in Nonconformist church registers, but in many cases no records can be found because no registers have survived. No duplicate records similar to bishop's transcripts were kept.

Most surviving Nonconformist registers before 1837 were deposited with the Registrar General in the nineteenth century, and are now held at TNA in series RG 4 and RG 8. The names of congregations and places can be searched using the Discovery catalogue. The registers have been digitized by several different online search services, and can be searched by name. A small number of registers were not deposited with the Registrar General, but most of them have now been deposited in local archives, where they are usually available on microfilm. Name indexes have often been produced by individuals or local family history societies, but a few pre-1837 Nonconformist registers held in local archives may remain unindexed.

Information about church members has sometimes survived in other records, discussed below. If a Nonconformist family were reasonably prosperous it may be possible to identify one or more previous generations in the complete absence of baptism and burial records, using sources such as wills, deeds and Chancery Proceedings.

Church Books and Other Records

Many congregations kept a volume known as a *church book* in which administrative matters were recorded. The information recorded was very variable, but often included the appointment of ministers and elders, admission of new members and minutes of meetings, including disciplinary action taken against members. Some church books contain lists of members, and records were sometimes made when members transferred from one congregation to another. Church books may survive for periods for which no records of births or baptisms exist. Although church books rarely contain sufficient genealogical information to enable relationships to be established in the absence of church registers, they can often demonstrate an association between certain surnames and a particular congregation over several generations. Deeds relating to property owned by churches may include the names of more prominent church members.

Church books and other records of Nonconformist congregations are usually held in local archives. Transcripts of the church books of some congregations have been published by organizations such as local record societies and church historical societies.

THE SOCIETY OF FRIENDS (QUAKERS)

The Society of Friends was established in the middle of the seventeenth century and its members became known as Quakers. They rejected many practices of the Church of England and other Nonconformist denominations. Quakers did not baptize children, hold conventional church services or employ clergy. They called the buildings where they held their meetings for worship meeting houses rather than churches or chapels. Persecuted in their early years, by the early Georgian period Quakers had become a largely middle-class denomination adhering to a strict and disciplined lifestyle. People born into Quaker families were expected to marry other Quakers,

A Quaker meeting house and burial ground. Quaker record-keeping was more thorough and methodical than in most other Nonconformist denominations.

and those who 'married out' were disowned. The number of Quakers therefore gradually declined throughout the Georgian era.

The Quakers developed a hierarchical meeting structure and were renowned for the thoroughness of their record-keeping. Local meetings for worship were known as Particular Meetings, each of which held an associated business meeting known as a Preparative Meeting, which prepared business for the Monthly Meeting, at which representatives of all the meetings in the area met to discuss business matters. Monthly Meetings were grouped into Quarterly Meetings, covering a larger area of one or two counties.

Although most resources for researching Quaker ancestry are held in archives, the Library of the Society of Friends in London holds many published sources and a variety of name indexes. Further information on researching Quaker ancestors can be found in Milligan and Thomas (1999).

Registers of Births, Marriages, Deaths and Burials

Quakers did not practise baptism but recorded the births of children, usually including the names of both parents. Quakers also recorded deaths and burials, and most Quaker meeting houses had burial grounds. Age at death was sometimes recorded before 1776 and regularly after that.

From their foundation, Quakers refused to marry in 'steeple houses' and performed their own marriage ceremonies. Although there were some doubts about the legal validity of earlier Quaker marriages, between 1754 and 1837 the Quakers were the only Christian denomination permitted to perform their own marriage ceremonies under Hardwicke's Marriage Act. Because Quakers were expected to marry other Quakers, marriages were relatively common between couples who lived some distance apart, often in different counties. Many Quaker marriage records include the names of one or both parents. Quaker marriages took the form of a meeting for worship attended by the whole congregation, and some marriage records include the names of all those who were present.

All pre-1837 Quaker registers were deposited with the Registrar General in the nineteenth century and are now held at TNA in series RG 6. As a result of the hierarchical meeting structure, births, marriages and deaths were sometimes recorded in more than one register. These records have been digitized by several different online search services.

Before the original registers were deposited in the nineteenth century, their contents were copied into digests, with some minor details omitted. Two copies of each digest were made. One copy was kept by the relevant Monthly Meeting and is now usually held in a local archive. The second set of copies is now held at the Library of the Society of Friends in London. Microfilm copies are available at the Society of Genealogists. The digests provided an easier method of searching before the original registers were digitized, but their usefulness in this respect has now diminished.

Unlike other Nonconformists, for whom marriages and sometimes burials can often be found in Anglican parish registers, records of births, marriages and deaths of members of Quaker families are usually entirely absent from the records of the Church of England during the Georgian era. The first appearance of a person with Quaker ancestry in a Georgian parish register was often their marriage to a non-Quaker, after which they were disowned. Because so many records were kept, many of which have survived, researching Quaker ancestry can be relatively straightforward. Even when registers have been lost, genealogical relationships between Quakers, who were mainly from a middle-class background, can often be established from other sources.

Quakers did not use the names of months, but referred to each month by its number. January only became 'first month' after the change to the Gregorian calendar in 1752. 'First month' had been March according to the Julian Calendar. 28th day of 3rd month 1739 was therefore 28th May 1739, and not 28th March. Quaker dates in pre-1752 records have often been recorded incorrectly in transcripts and indexes when this system has not been understood.

Quaker Minutes

Most issues and decisions concerning members of the Society of Friends were dealt with by Monthly Meetings. These included disciplinary matters, preliminaries before the marriage of members, including obtaining consent of parents and other relations and safeguarding the position of children from earlier marriages, and making regular payments to members in need. Members could be disowned for 'marrying out' or for moral offences. The Quakers had an elaborate system for providing references for members moving to other areas. Monthly Meetings issued certificates to members to take with them to their new Monthly Meeting and the issuing and receipt of certificates was recorded in the minutes. Quakers kept detailed minutes of their business meetings. Most Quaker minutes have been deposited in local archives, and their locations are listed on the Quaker Family History Society website.

METHODISTS

The Nonconformist groups established during the seventeenth century are often referred to collectively as *Old Dissent*, with the term *New Dissent* used for the various Methodist and similar groups that developed towards the end of the eighteenth century. Wesleyan Methodism began as a movement within the Church of England, and only became a separate denomination after the death of John Wesley in 1791. Most Methodists were Wesleyans, but a minority were Calvinists, and various other groups developed, such as the Primitive Methodists. Support for Methodism was strong among the lower class, particularly in areas where the Church of England was not well represented, which was mainly in industrial and urban areas. Although some Methodists were labourers, the majority were skilled workers.

Groups of Methodist churches were organized into *circuits*, and Methodist records often reflect this structure. Few Methodist birth and baptism registers exist before 1791, and the majority commence between 1810 and 1820. Burial registers are relatively rare. The Wesleyan Metropolitan Registry was established in 1818 for registering the births and baptisms of Wesleyan Methodists, and over 10,000 births and baptisms were recorded before 1837. These records, together with most other pre-1837 Methodist registers, were deposited with the Registrar General and have now been digitized. Other pre-1837 Methodist registers have subsequently been deposited in local archives.

Further information on researching Methodist ancestors can be found in Leary (2005) and Ratcliffe (2014).

OTHER PROTESTANT DENOMINATIONS

Various other Protestant denominations existed during the Georgian era, the most significant of which are discussed in this section. Most of their pre-1837 registers were deposited with the Registrar General, are held at TNA, and have now been digitized.

Several Huguenot congregations existed in England during the Georgian era. They had been founded by French Protestants escaping from persecution during the sixteenth and seventeenth centuries. As well as several congregations in London, there were also congregations in towns in the south of England and East Anglia, such as Canterbury, Southampton, Bristol, Plymouth and Norwich. The number of Huguenots gradually declined during the eighteenth century as they became anglicised and intermarried with members of other denominations. Transcripts of the church registers now held at TNA have been published by the Huguenot Society and are available on CD. Further information on researching Huguenot ancestors can be found in Currer-Briggs and Gambier (1985), and Chater (2012).

The Moravian Church originated in Bohemia in the fifteenth century, and congregations were established in England after 1740. Although early ministers were German, most church members were English. Congregations were established in London, and in towns such as Bristol, Bath, Malmesbury and Devonport. Moravian church registers are fairly detailed: place of birth was sometimes recorded in burial registers, for example. The Moravians kept detailed registers of members, which usually recorded date and place of birth, occupation, and date of death or leaving the congregation. Surviving membership records are held at the archives of the Moravian Church in London, and in other archives referred to on its website.

The Inghamites were established by Benjamin Ingham, and several congregations were established from the mid-eighteenth century, mainly in Lancashire and Yorkshire. Further information on researching Inghamite ancestors can be found in Oates (2003).

The New Church (whose members were also known as New Jerusalemites or Swedenborgians) was established in England in 1784 by disciples of the Swedish mystic Emanuel Swedenborg. A number of churches were established throughout the country, particularly in Lancashire. Early records of congregations are held at the Library of the Swedenborg Society in London.

ROMAN CATHOLICS

Although they were subject to various legal restrictions, by the early Georgian period most law-abiding English Catholics were left in peace. Their numbers remained very small during the eighteenth century. Catholics were concentrated in areas with Catholic gentry, mainly in the north of England, and particularly in Lancashire. Before the 1780s most Catholic priests were either chaplains to gentry families or peripatetic. An Act of 1778 removed some restrictions on Catholics, and freed priests from prosecution. A further Act of 1791 permitted chapels to be built, and the Catholic Relief Act of 1829 removed many other restrictions. The number of Roman Catholics began to grow after 1791 as a result of the opening of a large number of new chapels, immigration from France after the French Revolution, and immigration from Ireland. In the early nineteenth century the most significant factor in the growth of Catholicism was immigration from Ireland. The Georgian era therefore witnessed the transformation of English Catholicism from a faith adhered to by a small number of gentry and their tenants in rural areas into a much larger denomination dominated by lower-class families in urban areas.

Registers of Baptisms and Burials

Relatively few pre-1837 Roman Catholic church registers were deposited with the Registrar General in the nineteenth century.

Those deposited, held at TNA in series RG 4, were mainly from Northumberland, Durham and Yorkshire. Most early registers have now been deposited in local archives (record offices) or Roman Catholic archdiocesan archives in Westminster and Birmingham. The Catholic Record Society was established in 1904 and has published transcriptions of many registers. Some of the earlier volumes are now out of copyright, so have been digitized and are freely available on the internet. Other transcripts have been published by the Catholic Family History Society and local family history societies. All Catholic registers known to exist for the Georgian era have been listed in a set of regional volumes by Gandy (1993), which can be found in major libraries. In 2017 Findmypast reached an agreement with the Catholic Church to digitize church records to create the *Catholic Heritage Archive,* and records are gradually being added.

Many Catholic registers are in Latin, but the entries are usually in a standard format. Baptism registers usually include the name of godparents (known as 'sponsors'). Although Catholics were required to marry in the Church of England before 1837, some couples also went through Catholic marriage ceremonies, which were recorded in Catholic registers that may include additional genealogical information.

Lists of Papists

Roman Catholics were referred to in official documents as papists, recusants or popish recusants. Lists of papists were made for various purposes throughout the eighteenth century, and can often be found in Quarter Sessions records held in local archives. Some lists have been published. In 1767 Parliament required the numbers of Catholics throughout the country to be recorded. The records sent from dioceses are held at the Parliamentary Archives, and transcriptions in two volumes entitled *Returns of Papists, 1767* have been published by the Catholic Record Society (Worrall, 1980 and 1989). The amount of information included in these records varies according to the diocese. Records for the dioceses of Chester (Cheshire, Lancashire and parts of Cumberland, Westmorland and the North Riding of Yorkshire), Durham (Durham and Northumberland), Exeter (Devon and Cornwall) and Hereford (Herefordshire and part of Shropshire) include names, ages, occupations and the number of years each person had lived in their parish of residence. Records for the dioceses of York and Carlisle contain similar information, but include only the initials of individuals rather than their full names. However, the amount of information in these records, which are arranged by parish and then by household, may enable families to be identified when used in combination with other sources. The lists for other dioceses are summaries that include neither names nor initials, but some original parish lists that include names are held locally. Lists for Staffordshire, Derbyshire and parts of Shropshire and Warwickshire are held in the records of the Diocese of Lichfield, and transcriptions have been published. Similar lists are held in the records of the Dioceses of Salisbury, Oxford, Worcester and Norfolk. These records taken together provide a complete listing of the Catholic population in several counties in 1767, with over half of English Catholics at that time listed by name. The Catholic Family History Society's *Margaret Higgins Index of Catholics in England and their Friends 1607-1840* includes the names and details of over 250,000 Catholics, from a variety of sources, including the lists made in 1767.

Chapter 6

EDUCATION AND EMPLOYMENT

Records for a range of occupations have survived from the Georgian era, although the majority relate to skilled occupations and professions. These records can provide a perspective on ancestors' lives unavailable in other sources, and sometimes include information on parentage or birthplace. However, finding relevant information in such a diverse range of sources is not always straightforward. It can often be difficult to establish an individual's occupation in the first place, as this was not routinely recorded in church registers before 1813. Many occupational records are not searchable online and some have not been indexed at all, so finding relevant information may require visiting archives and browsing page by page through original handwritten records, or paying to have research carried out.

This chapter provides an outline of the educational and employment records that have survived for people who lived in Georgian England. Records relating to service in the army, navy and militia are discussed in the next chapter. Many books are available on researching ancestors with particular occupations, which are referred to in the relevant sections.

EDUCATION

The state was not involved in the provision of education until compulsory elementary education was introduced in the middle of the Victorian era. Some lower-class children received an elementary education in parish or charity schools, but only a very small proportion, mainly boys, were educated at secondary level or above.

It was normal practice in the past to teach writing only after children had learned to read, so an inability to write was not necessarily an indication of being unable to read.

Many boys from the gentry and aristocracy had private tutors, and girls in middle- and upper-class families learned 'accomplishments' at home, such as speaking French and playing the piano. Schools providing secondary-level education consisted of what are now public schools, such as Eton and Winchester, which educated the sons of the gentry and aristocracy, and endowed grammar schools, which served their local area and educated mainly middle-class boys and the sons of more prosperous tradesmen. Many of these schools, or their successor institutions, are still in existence, and their historical records have often survived. Some schools maintain their own archives, but other historical school records have been deposited in public archives. Some lists of former pupils have been published, which usually include dates of admission and often details of parentage. The Society of Genealogists holds a large collection of published school registers. Many older published lists have been digitized and are available through Google Books, the Internet Archive and online subscription services.

Oxford and Cambridge were the only universities in England until 1832. A university degree was usually necessary for ordination in the Church of England, and attending university enabled younger sons of the aristocracy and gentry to obtain livings in parishes where their families held the right to appoint incumbents.

The surviving records of the universities of Oxford and Cambridge and their constituent colleges are extensive. Information on former students has been compiled in two multi-volume works entitled *Alumni Oxonienses* and *Alumni Cantabrigienses*, both of which can be found in libraries and archives and also searched online. *ACAD (A Cambridge Alumni Database)* is a corrected and updated online version of the information in the Cambridge volumes maintained by the University of Cambridge. Entries in alumni lists usually include the date of admission to the university (matriculation), the age when admitted, the place of birth and father's name, and the degree awarded. The Cambridge alumni records contain more detail

Wadham College, Oxford. Oxford and Cambridge were the only universities in England until 1832.

than those for Oxford, sometimes including information obtained from other sources relating to subsequent careers, often within the Church of England. Lists of alumni of some individual Oxford and Cambridge colleges have been published, usually containing more information than the university lists.

During the Georgian era, men who did not subscribe to the teachings of the Church of England were unable to graduate from Oxford or Cambridge or enter certain professions. Dissenting academies were established throughout the country which combined the roles of grammar school and university and provided both a general education for boys and training for men wishing to become Nonconformist ministers. Information on dissenting academies is now being collected in a project coordinated by Queen Mary University of London. *Dissenting Academies Online* contains information on students and teachers, including some genealogical information, compiled from a variety of sources.

IDENTIFYING OCCUPATIONS

The father's occupation was only routinely recorded in baptism registers from 1813 onwards. Occupation was also recorded sporadically in baptism, marriage and burial registers before that date. It is advisable to look at records for whole families and not just those for direct ancestors. If a couple had seven children, all baptized before 1813, the father's occupation might have been recorded in one of the baptism records. It is therefore always advisable to consult the full records, rather relying on index records containing only names.

The occupations of people who survived beyond the Georgian era were recorded in death registration records from 1837 and census records from 1841. Death registration records for widows usually included the names and occupations of their husbands, who could have died several decades before 1837. Occupation may also have been recorded in a range of other sources discussed in this book, including marriage licence bonds and allegations, wills, deeds, Poor Law records, other parish records such as Overseers' and Churchwardens' accounts, records of the secular and church courts, poll books, and lists of apprentices and freemen.

Printed trade directories for towns and cities were published from the mid-eighteenth century onwards, listing tradesmen, such as blacksmiths, tailors and bakers, as well as gentry, clergy, lawyers, surgeons and apothecaries. The coverage of directories gradually spread to rural areas from the early nineteenth century. Directories relevant to the Georgian era for areas outside London can be identified using Norton (1984), a standard reference work often available in local studies libraries and archives. London directories can be identified using Atkins (1990). Historical directories can be found in archives and local studies libraries, but many have now been digitized and are freely available through a variety of websites, including Google Books, the Internet Archive and the *Historical Directories of England and Wales* collection, part of the University of Leicester's Special Collections Online.

Most occupations recorded in Georgian sources relate to men, as women were usually referred to in records in relation to their husbands or fathers. Although increasingly disapproved of by the Victorian middle class, in the eighteenth century and earlier it was not uncommon for women to assist their husbands in running businesses. Some widows continued and even expanded businesses after the deaths of their husbands, employing workers and servants, and acting as masters to apprentices.

SKILLED OCCUPATIONS: APPRENTICES AND FREEMEN

Most skilled occupations were entered through voluntary apprenticeships, involving the parents of a child, usually a boy, paying a sum of money to a master to enable the child to learn a trade for a fixed number of years. Girls were also apprenticed, in trades such as dressmaking, sometimes referred to as mantua-making, and millinery. Children were usually apprenticed around the age of 14, for a term of seven years, with the apprenticeship lasting until at least the age of 21. Apprenticeships were undertaken to enter not only skilled trades and crafts, but also some occupations that are now regarded as professions, such as surgery and the law. Parish apprenticeships, under the Poor Law, were quite different, and are discussed in Chapter 9.

An apprenticeship was made legally binding by means of an *indenture*: a contract between two parties written on a sheet of parchment with a wavy (indentured) edge. Indentures were produced by writing the contract twice on a single sheet of parchment and then cutting it into two pieces, with one copy given to each party. Cutting with a wavy edge ensured that the authenticity of documents could later be confirmed if necessary by fitting the parts together.

Many apprenticeships were undertaken without the expense and formality of an indenture. Men often apprenticed their own sons, and successive generations of blacksmiths and tailors can often be found living in the same village without any evidence of indentures having been drawn up. Apprenticeship by indenture was common in towns and cities, as serving an apprenticeship could enable men to become *freemen*, sometimes known as *burgesses* (a term also used to refer to MPs representing boroughs). Few apprentice indentures have survived, but some have been preserved in the records of guilds and livery companies and others in collections of family papers.

Stamp Duty was imposed on apprenticeship indentures from 1710 to 1811. The payments were recorded in *Board of Stamps: Apprenticeship Books*, held at TNA in series IR 1. For each apprentice the name, abode and trade of the master, the name of the apprentice and the date of the indenture were recorded. These records are now searchable online through several different online subscription services, reflecting their importance in family history research. The names of the fathers of apprentices were recorded before 1752, but only rarely after that date. The earlier records are therefore particularly valuable in establishing parentage.

Apprenticeships in cities and towns were usually controlled by craft guilds or the corporations of cities and boroughs. After completing an apprenticeship men could apply to become freemen, which gave a range of privileges, sometimes including voting rights in parliamentary elections. Freedom could also be obtained by patrimony (if the father was a freeman) or by redemption (purchase), and sometimes by marrying the widow or daughter of a freeman. Registers of apprentice admissions usually recorded the father's name, abode and occupation. Registers of freemen usually recorded how the freedom was obtained, and when obtained by patrimony often include the name of the father. Apprenticeship and freedom records in combination can therefore sometimes enable several generations of an ancestral line to be established.

Surviving records of guilds and corporations are usually held in local archives, and may include apprenticeship admission registers, copies of apprenticeship indentures and records of freedom admissions. Extensive collections of guild records have survived for some towns and cities, such as Newcastle upon Tyne, held at Tyne & Wear Archives. Lists for some areas have been published, such as *A Calendar of the Registers of Apprentices of the City of Gloucester 1700-1834* published by Bristol & Gloucestershire Archaeological Society, and *Exeter Freemen 1266-1967* published by Devon & Cornwall Record Society.

Apprenticeships in London were controlled by *livery companies.* Most historical records of livery companies are held at the Guildhall Library in the City of London, although some are still held by the companies themselves. The surviving apprenticeship records of many livery companies were originally abstracted by Cliff Webb and published in a series of separate pamphlets, which may be found in libraries, but are now searchable on Findmypast in a database entitled *London Apprenticeship Abstracts 1442-1850.* A dedicated website, *The Records of London's Livery Companies Online (ROLLCO),* has been established to provide a searchable database of livery company membership records, and currently includes the records of several companies. The trades in which people were apprenticed and the livery companies of which they became members were sometimes completely different, so people can be found in the records of livery companies quite unrelated to their occupations.

Becoming a freeman of the City of London required first obtaining the freedom of a livery company. Freedom by patrimony could be obtained only if the father had been made a freeman before the son was born. Freedom admission papers for the City, many of which consist of apprenticeship indentures, are held at London Metropolitan Archives and have been digitized by Ancestry. The majority of apprentices in provincial towns were from the surrounding area, but a significant proportion of London apprentices were from outside the capital and many came from some distance away. London apprenticeship records and freedom admission papers can therefore enable the place of birth to be established of many people who lived in London but had not been born there. Further information on researching freemen of the City of London can be found in Aldous (1999).

Few records of employment were kept after individuals had completed their apprenticeships or become freemen, but apprenticeship records included masters' names, so they can provide an indication of the range of years during which masters engaged apprentices and the numbers they employed. References to individual tradesmen may also be found in the minute books of guilds, livery companies and corporations, particularly relating to those tradesmen who occupied official positions.

Further information about apprenticeship records can be found in Raymond (2010).

RECORDS OF SPECIFIC OCCUPATIONS

Few records have survived relating to the employment of unskilled workers such as industrial or agricultural labourers, or the increasing number of people who worked in factories during the Industrial Revolution. Some records of servants, both indoor domestic servants and outdoor servants such as grooms and gamekeepers, have survived in the records of landowning families. Records are more likely to have survived for people employed in occupations that required either education or serving an apprenticeship, the main sources for which have been discussed earlier in this chapter. The occupations for which further information is most likely to be available are discussed in this section.

Servants

Landowning families employed a range of indoor and outdoor servants. Indoor servants included butlers, footmen, valets, housekeepers, cooks, kitchen maids, laundry maids, parlour maids and lady's maids. Outdoor servants, mainly men and boys, included gardeners, grooms, coachmen, stable boys and gamekeepers. Accounts of expenditure and records of employees were kept and some of these historical records still exist, but from the researcher's perspective whether anything can be found relating to their ancestors is usually a matter of chance. While historical records survive in profusion for some landowning families, many 'old records' no longer perceived as being of any value were undoubtedly recycled during the paper salvage drives of the two world wars. Even when records have survived, finding references to specific ancestors is rarely straightforward, as it is dependent on ascertaining that they were, or were likely to have been, employed by a particular family. This type of research is the complete antithesis of modern 'internet genealogy'. It is time-consuming and can often be fruitless, but can also be very rewarding when the minutiae of ancestors' daily lives can be observed in such records, as in the following example.

Several generations of families with the surname Boaler lived in the parish of Laughton en le Morthen in the West Riding of Yorkshire during the eighteenth century. Various clues suggested that some family members might have been employed at Sandbeck Park, a landed estate that became the seat of the Earls of Scarbrough (*sic*) in the early eighteenth century and is still in that family's possession. Specific references to Sandbeck Park appeared in some records, and subsequent generations of the Boaler family were employed in similar roles by the Dukes of Portland at Welbeck Abbey in Nottinghamshire. An extensive collection of historical records is still held at Sandbeck Park and may be consulted by arrangement. Accounts include many references to payments made to members of the Boaler family between 1759 and 1771. Joseph Boaler, later employed by the Duke of Portland as a gamekeeper, married Martha Burgoyne in 1771, and they left Sandbeck Park around the same time. The accounts also include many references to the Burgoyne family, including wages paid to Martha Burgoyne between 1769 and 1771.

It was common for several members of the same family to be employed by landowning families, sometimes over several generations, so records may contain clues to relationships or corroborate those that could only be regarded as tentative based on the information in parish registers. However, the main value of such detailed records is in a family history context, as they can paint a vivid picture of the daily lives of ancestors engaged in occupations for which surviving records are usually minimal.

If it appears likely that an ancestor was employed by a landowning family, families with properties in specific areas can be identified using local histories and county histories. These are available in local studies libraries, and similar information can often be found online. Record collections relating to landowning families, formerly included in the National Register of Archives, can now be identified by selecting the Advanced Search mode of TNA's Discovery catalogue, selecting *Record creators* and searching for the family name. The majority of collections of family papers are now held in public archives, although not necessarily in the area where properties were located, and a small proportion remain in private hands.

Because servants often moved between their employers' estates, establishing that landowners owned properties in specific areas can provide corroborating evidence that baptism records for children with the same parents' names in those areas actually relate to the same parents.

Gamekeepers

From 1710 the number of gamekeepers was restricted to one per manor, with the names recorded by the Clerk of the Peace. From 1785 all gamekeepers' deputations, recording the appointment of gamekeepers, were required to be registered with the Clerk of the Peace, with certificates renewed yearly. These records, when they survive, can be found in Quarter Sessions records in local archives. Lists of gamekeepers were often published in local newspapers, many of which can now be searched online via the *British Newspaper Archive*. Successive generations of the same family often served as gamekeepers, so the names recorded can sometimes provide clues to genealogical relationships. Details relating to the employment of gamekeepers can sometimes be found in the records of landowning families (discussed above). The names of gamekeepers may appear in newspaper reports of court proceedings against poachers.

Innkeepers

Innkeepers, otherwise known as alehouse keepers or publicans, were required to be licensed by the local Justices of the Peace. From 1753 to 1828 the law required Clerks of the Peace to keep registers of *alehouse recognizances*, although some counties had kept such records earlier. Recognizances were bonds for good behaviour signed by alehouse keepers and one or two bondsmen. Surviving records usually consist of annual *recognizance rolls*, which list the names of individuals to whom licences had been issued and their bondsmen. These records are one of the few sources of occupational information in which women are listed alongside men.

Recognizance rolls, when they survive, can be found in Quarter Sessions records in local archives. Widows often took over the running of inns after the deaths of their husbands, and licensing records may demonstrate that an inn passed through the hands of several members of the same family.

Merchant Seamen

Systematic records of merchant seamen only began to be kept by the Board of Trade in 1835. These records are now held at TNA and have been digitized by Findmypast. Some of these records, relating to the issue of *seamen's tickets*, include date of birth and birthplace. Although many of the men listed were young, some older men who had died before the 1851 census were included, enabling dates and places of birth as early as the 1770s to be traced.

Various other sources are available that may include detailed information about specific seamen, particularly those whose widows or families applied for charitable assistance after their deaths. The Corporation of Trinity House helped seamen and their dependants in need, and applications often include evidence of baptisms and marriages. These and other Trinity House records are now held by the Society of Genealogists. Indexes can be searched on Findmypast, and copies of original records can be obtained from the Society. Further information about these records, and the relatively small number of other sources existing for merchant seamen in the Georgian era, can be found in Smith et al. (1998) and Watts and Watts (2002).

Post Office Employees

The General Post Office was established in the seventeenth century, and by the beginning of the Georgian era there was a growing network of routes connecting London to post offices in large and small towns throughout the country. Historical records are held at the Postal Museum Archive in London. Those relevant to the Georgian era comprise Establishment Books from 1691 and Staff Nomination and Appointment books from 1737. The latter collection has been digitized by Ancestry. Most of the records are for more senior employees.

Police

Police forces did not exist for most of the Georgian era. Rural areas relied on unpaid Parish Constables and many towns and cities employed paid constables and watchmen. The army and militia were used to deal with riots and civil disturbances. The Metropolitan Police was established in 1829, and early records of appointments are held at TNA. Some borough police forces were established following the Municipal Corporations Act of 1835, but the establishment of local police forces did not become compulsory until 1856.

Civil and Crown Servants

The Civil Service was relatively small during the Georgian era, as the role of national government was much more limited than it is today. Personnel records of government employees were not routinely kept. Civil servants are listed in the *Royal Kalendar* from 1767 and the *British Imperial Calendar* from 1809. A set of volumes is available at TNA, some have been digitized on the Internet Archive, and many have been filmed by the LDS. A collection of records originally held by the Civil Service containing birth and baptism records, mainly after 1800, is held by the Society of Genealogists, and these records are now available on Findmypast.

Records of employees of the Royal Household are held at the Royal Archives at Windsor Castle and at TNA. Many of the records held by the Royal Archives of interest to family history researchers are now available on Findmypast. Records held at TNA mainly relate to employees of the Lord Chamberlain and Lord Steward and have not been digitized. Further information can be found in a research guide on TNA's website.

Customs and Excise Officers

The Customs and Excise were two separate bodies during the Georgian era. Surviving records of both are held at TNA. Customs and Excise officers had to be both literate and numerate, and it was common practice for brothers and sons of existing officers to enter the relevant service.

Customs officers were based in coastal areas and ports and were responsible for collecting duties on imported and exported goods, as well as for preventing smuggling before 1822. They had a range of job titles, such as Tide Waiter and Waterman, although the latter term could also refer to a boatman on an inland waterway. Surviving sources include quarterly Establishment Books which list all employees by location.

Excise officers were responsible for collecting duties on domestically-produced goods, even when some or all of the ingredients had been imported. Duties were paid on goods such as beer, wine, spirits, tea, coffee, salt, sugar, soap, candles and tobacco, which were produced throughout the country. Excise officers were therefore based in all areas, and men often changed location several times during their careers. Minute books record the posting of officers throughout the Georgian era, and Entry Papers from 1820 onwards record the dates and places of birth of new entrants.

With the exception of the Entry Papers for the Excise, surviving records do not include genealogical information such as birthplace or parentage, but they can enable the locations where men served to be established. This information can provide corroborating evidence that baptism records with the same parents' names in different areas relate to the same parents, and may enable other baptisms in previously unidentified locations to be identified. Minute books also include details of promotions, illnesses, accidents and disciplinary matters.

Information on the range of records available for researching the careers of Customs and Excise officers can be found on TNA's website. Using these records requires either visiting TNA in person or employing a researcher. However, the handwritten name indexes to the individual Excise Board minute books (CUST 47) have been digitized and can be browsed via the Discovery catalogue, enabling relevant volumes to be identified in advance. Although they can be time-consuming to search, if it can be established from other sources that a man served in the Customs or Excise it is almost certain that some worthwhile information will be found in these records.

Lawyers: Barristers, Attorneys, Solicitors and Proctors

Lawyer is a generic term referring to members of the legal profession. There were three major categories of lawyer practising in the civil courts during the Georgian era: *barristers, attorneys* and *solicitors.*

Barristers were usually of a higher social status than attorneys and solicitors, and included some men from upper-class backgrounds. They provided expert advice and advocacy and had a monopoly over representing people in the higher courts. Attorneys represented clients in legal proceedings in the courts of common law and solicitors represented clients in the courts of equity. Lawyers performing duties similar to attorneys and solicitors in the ecclesiastical courts were known as *proctors*.

The number of barristers was relatively small and in 1780 there were only about 230. To practise as a barrister required several years' training at one of the four Inns of Court in London: Gray's Inn, Lincoln's Inn, Inner Temple and Middle Temple. Admission registers for all four Inns were kept, and are now available online, either as searchable databases or as digitized images of earlier published volumes. They record date of admission and father's name and abode.

To practise as an attorney or solicitor after 1729 required working for five years with a qualified lawyer as an articled clerk. Articles were subject to Stamp Duty, so records can often be found in the Apprenticeship Books referred to earlier in this chapter. There is no single source of information for attorneys and solicitors, but details relating to their admission may be found in the records of courts in which they practised, which are held at TNA. Some of these records include information on parentage. Many names in these records are searchable via the Discovery catalogue and some records relating to articles of clerkship have been digitized by Ancestry. Further information on the range of sources available for attorneys and solicitors can be found on TNA's website. Admissions of proctors were recorded in records of the church courts, which are held in the archives holding the records of relevant dioceses and archdeaconries.

Further information on researching lawyers can be found in Holborn (1999), Brooks and Herber (2006) and Wade (2010).

Medical Practitioners: Physicians, Surgeons and Apothecaries

The medical practitioners of the Georgian era were divided into three categories: *physicians* who diagnosed internal disorders, *surgeons* who performed operations, and *apothecaries* who prepared medicines.

Physicians were relatively few in number and were highly educated, often holding degrees, but not necessarily from Oxford or Cambridge. Some had attended universities in Scotland (St Andrews, Aberdeen, Glasgow and Edinburgh) or Ireland (Trinity College, Dublin) or in continental Europe. Physicians were generally of higher social status than surgeons and apothecaries, and many were members of the Royal College of Physicians. Biographies of Fellows and Licentiates were compiled by William Munk in the nineteenth century, and volumes have continued to be published, entitled *The Roll of the Royal College of Physicians of London*, commonly known as *Munk's Roll*. The biographies often include details of birthplace, parentage and career. This information is being made available online by the Royal College of Physicians through the *Lives of the Fellows* website.

Surgeons and apothecaries generally served apprenticeships, so may be found in sources discussed earlier in this chapter. Records from many relevant sources have been extracted and published in *Eighteenth Century Medics* (Wallis and Wallis, 1988).

Some records relating to surgeons may be found in the records of barber-surgeons companies. Before 1745 many surgeons in London were members of the Barber-Surgeons Company, but that year the surgeons split from the barbers, and later became the Royal College of Surgeons. Barber-surgeons companies are known to have existed in over twenty English towns. The few records that survive include those for Chester and Newcastle upon Tyne, where barber-surgeons were combined with wax- and tallow-chandlers.

Various published directories of medical practitioners are available covering the Georgian era, but they rarely include any genealogical information. A wide range of resources is held at the Wellcome Library in London, and information can be found on its website. Further information on researching medical practitioners can be found in Bourne and Chicken (1994) and Higgs (2011).

Church of England Clergymen

Anglican clergymen were also known as *clerks in holy orders* or simply as *clerks*. Before the nineteenth century the description 'clerk', without any further elaboration, usually referred to a clergyman. Clerks involved in record-keeping were more likely to be referred to in relation to their function, such as 'Clerk in the Navy Office'. A clerk in holy orders should not be confused with a *Parish Clerk*, who was a layman appointed in each parish with a range of religious and administrative duties. Until the nineteenth century most clergymen were Oxford or Cambridge graduates, so can be found in the lists of alumni referred to above. Their names often appear in records followed by the post-nominal letters A.B. or A.M., short for Artium Baccalaureus and Artium Magister (Bachelor of Arts and Master of Arts).

Applicants for ordination were required to submit references and evidence of baptism. Ordination papers have often survived in the records of the diocese in which ordination took place. Diocesan records are discussed in Chapter 4. Lists of clergy for some counties have been published, such as *Northamptonshire and Rutland Clergy from 1500,* and generally include more information than university alumni lists. The *Clergy of the Church of England Database* (CCEd) is a project to collect information on the careers of clergymen from a large number of original sources held in archives throughout the country. Its associated website is freely available.

Further information on researching Anglican clergymen can be found in Towey (2006) and the relevant chapter of Raymond (2017b).

Nonconformist Ministers

The main Nonconformist denominations employing ministers throughout the Georgian era were Presbyterians, Independents (Congregationalists) and Baptists. Methodists also employed ministers from the late eighteenth century onwards. The Quakers did not employ ministers. Finding information about Nonconformist ministers may require searching a range of sources held in specific archives, so knowledge of the history of relevant denominations and the location of their records is essential.

Some Nonconformist ministers were educated at dissenting academies (discussed above). Biographical accounts and obituaries of ministers were sometimes written in church minute books, discussed in Chapter 5. *The Surman Index Online* is a biographical index of

Congregational and Presbyterian ministers made available by Queen Mary University of London. Records of the various Nonconformist denominations which may include information about ministers are described in Mullett (1991) and Raymond (2017a).

Chapter 7

WAR AND PEACE

The Victorian era was a period of relative peace, during which no wars were fought against other Western European nations. This was in sharp contrast to the Georgian era, when wars were relatively frequent, and mainly involved France. Although it is quite common for family history researchers to discover no direct ancestors serving in the armed forces during the Victorian era, it is likely that almost everyone has ancestors who served in the army, militia or navy during the Georgian era. Not only were wars more frequent, but also the number of ancestors in each previous generation doubles, with a corresponding doubling in the number of male ancestors living at any one time. Britain was at war with France almost continuously from 1793 to 1815, a period far longer than the world wars of the twentieth century, and some of the men who fought at Waterloo in 1815 had not been born in 1793.

A wide range of sources is available at TNA for researching Georgian ancestors who served in the armed forces. They can be subdivided into two major categories: records relating to individuals, such as pension records, and records relating to military units, mainly army battalions and ships, in which individuals were listed, such as muster rolls and pay lists. Many of the records relating to individuals have now been indexed or digitized, but they exist for only a proportion of soldiers and a relatively small number of sailors. It may be possible to follow a man's military service using sources such as muster rolls, but this requires becoming familiar with the records and spending time at TNA, or alternatively employing a specialist researcher. Searching records of this type is dependent not only on finding clues that a man served in the army or navy but also on establishing the identity of his regiment or ship.

This chapter provides an overview of the armed forces of the Georgian era and outlines the sources available for researching men's careers. Bevan (2006) describes sources available at TNA in general and specialist books have been written on researching ancestors who served in the army, navy and Royal Marines. Those books are referred to in the relevant sections below.

GEORGIAN WARS

Although the Georgian era began and ended with periods of peace, between 1739 and 1815 there were more years of war than years of peace. The major wars were as follows:

1739–48	War of Jenkins' Ear (1739–48) and War of the Austrian Succession (1740–8)
1756–63	Seven Years War
1775–83	American War of Independence and war with France (1778–83)
1793–1802	French Revolutionary War
1803–15	Napoleonic War and war with the United States (1812–15)

Eighteenth-century wars between European powers before 1793 have been described by some historians as 'restrained' and 'limited', as armies were small and many contained contingents of foreign mercenaries. However, the wars from 1793 to 1815 were on a scale that would not be experienced again until the First World War. This prolonged period of conflict had a greater impact on the population in general than the Industrial Revolution that was taking place at the same time. Following the resumption of war in 1803 after a brief interval of peace, Britain was at a greater risk of invasion than at any time until 1940. During the century following the Battle of Waterloo, the period from 1793 to 1815 was referred to as the 'Great War'. Most families had one or more members serving in the armed forces and many lost relatives in battle or through disease.

Few war memorials were erected, but memorials to men who had served were sometimes placed in churches and churchyards by their families, although the majority were for officers, as might be expected. Bromley and Bromley (2011) contains the recorded memorials to 3,000 men who served in the Peninsula War and at Waterloo, and other memorials may be found in miscellaneous collections of recorded inscriptions.

Evidence of Military Service

Enlisting in the army or navy, particularly during peacetime, could be an attractive option for some lower-class men compared to the work that was available locally. Although the pay was low, a bounty was paid on volunteering, men were supplied with regular food and drink, and service in the navy offered the possibility of prize money when enemy ships were captured. At a time when most people from lower-class backgrounds rarely travelled very far, enlisting in the army or navy offered young men the opportunity to leave home and see the wider world. The army and navy also provided an opportunity for men from middle- and upper-class backgrounds to pursue careers as officers.

Occupation was not routinely recorded in parish registers before 1813, and afterwards only in baptism registers. However, even if occupation had been recorded, a significant proportion of soldiers and sailors, particularly in the period from 1793 to 1815, were young unmarried men who served for the duration of the war and were then discharged, so no relevant records would have appeared in parish registers in any case. Some men were only away from home for a few years, but others for much longer. Although the evidence of military service that can be found in sources other than military records tends to be minimal, clues can often be found by examining the course of men's lives.

Although men could marry at any age, a late marriage could be an indication of earlier military service. A long gap between the baptisms of children during wartime is also a clue to military service. A couple marrying in 1802, with children baptized in the same area in 1803, 1805, 1814, 1816, 1818 and 1820, suggests a prolonged period of absence between 1805 and 1814. Although many wives of soldiers and militiamen stayed at home, some did accompany their husbands, so further baptisms may be found in unexpected locations.

Some men met their future wives while serving away from home, married in the bride's parish, and later returned to their home areas with their wives. Marriages that cannot be found in men's home areas could have taken place in completely different parts of the country, particularly in areas with military encampments or garrisons. Some soldiers married while serving in Ireland, but the majority of Church of Ireland registers were destroyed in 1922, so it is unlikely that relevant marriage records will be found.

It is often entirely coincidental that a series of baptism records of children with the same parents' names in different parts of the country appear to relate to members of the same family, but the probability that they actually were increases during wartime. Evidence that soldiers were serving in the areas where marriages or baptisms were recorded can be found by searching army and militia muster rolls.

If men's burials cannot be found in their home parishes it is possible that they died away from home while serving in the army, militia or navy. The dates and locations of death of soldiers and sailors can be found in muster rolls, but searching them requires knowing the name of the regiment or ship.

Clues that men served in the armed forces between 1793 and 1815 can often be obtained from the birthplaces of children recorded in the 1851 and later censuses. Military service may provide an explanation of why ancestors or their siblings were born in unusual or unexpected locations, particularly in areas that had a strong military presence at the time. The 1841 census enables children born outside of England to be identified.

Some registers of births and baptisms, marriages, and deaths and burials, relating to men serving in the armed forces from the late eighteenth century onwards, both at home and abroad, are held by the GRO, referred to as *Regimental registers*, *Army returns* and *Chaplains' returns*. Indexes are available on microfiche in some libraries and archives, and these indexes can also be searched on Findmypast as *British Nationals Armed Forces Births/Marriages/Deaths*.

It is necessary to purchase certificates to access the information in these records. Not all marriages included in the Regimental registers have been indexed, but the GRO will carry out a search if details of the regiment and the approximate date are provided.

THE ARMY

The combat arms of the British army were the infantry, cavalry and artillery, with the vast majority of men serving in numbered infantry regiments, known as Regiments of Foot. In 1782 it was decided that infantry regiments should be associated with particular areas, so the 68th Regiment of Foot became the 68th (Durham) Regiment of Foot, for example. However, regiments continued to recruit throughout the country, so the name of a regiment rarely provides any indication of a soldier's origins.

The fighting unit of the infantry was the battalion. Most regiments had only one battalion, but some had two or more, particularly during wartime, which usually served in different locations. Infantry battalions had a full-strength complement of about 1,000 men, but actual strength was often much less. Battalions, commanded by lieutenant colonels, were usually divided into ten companies, each under the command of a captain or major. Cavalry regiments were fewer in number and smaller than infantry regiments.

The British army was relatively small in comparison with the armies of France, Prussia, Austria and Russia. The largest theatre of operations during the French Revolutionary and Napoleonic Wars was the Iberian Peninsula between 1808 and 1814, where the British army fought alongside Portuguese and Spanish allies. Although the Battle of Waterloo in 1815 is often celebrated as a British victory, only 23,000 of the 67,000 men in Wellington's army were British, and they were joined towards the end of the battle by 50,000 Prussians.

As well as deaths in battle, deaths from illnesses and infected wounds were common. Service in the West Indies was particularly hazardous as a result of mosquito-borne diseases such as yellow fever and malaria. The mortality rate in garrisons in Jamaica was seven times that in Canada. In 1809 a force of 40,000 men landed on the island of Walcheren in the Netherlands, but within a few weeks over 60 per cent had succumbed to 'Walcheren fever', now believed to be a combination of malaria, typhus, typhoid and dysentery. Over 4,000 men died and many of those who survived took years to recover.

In social composition the Georgian army reflected the English country estate. Many commissioned officers were the sons of country gentlemen and the majority of soldiers were from labouring or other relatively low-status occupations. However, the possibility of promotion to corporal or sergeant provided many lower-class men with an opportunity for advancement that would rarely have been available in civilian life. Promotion to officer from the ranks was rare, but some sergeants became officers during wartime.

The East India Company maintained its own armies from the mid-eighteenth century. Most regiments consisted of Indian soldiers commanded by British officers, but some regiments were composed entirely of Europeans. The armies of the East India Company are not discussed further in this book, but information on the records available can be found in Bailey (2006).

Further information on researching army ancestors can be found in Spencer (2008), Watts and Watts (2009), and Fowler (2017).

Soldiers

Soldiers generally enlisted for life, but limited service of seven years in the infantry, or ten years in the cavalry or artillery, was introduced in 1806. From the perspective of the information that is likely to be available (but is not necessarily easy to find), soldiers can be divided into three broad categories: those who died while serving as soldiers, those who were discharged with pensions for injury or long service, and those who were discharged without pensions. Army recruitment increased significantly during wartime, particularly between 1793 and 1815, but when hostilities ended many men who had served for relatively short periods and had not been injured were discharged without receiving pensions.

Records of the award of pensions were kept by the Royal Hospital, Chelsea, which had been established as a place of residence for soldiers who had been wounded and were disabled, or were aged and infirm. Residents were known as *in-pensioners*, but Chelsea Hospital was also responsible for paying pensions to non-residents known as *out-pensioners,* who greatly outnumbered in-pensioners. As well as for illness and disability, pensions were also awarded for long service, usually of at least twenty years, with the reason for discharge generally being recorded as 'worn out'. The description *out-pensioner* or *Chelsea Pensioner* in non-military records indicates that a man had served as a soldier and been awarded a pension. Individual pension records survive for many soldiers from the 1760s onwards, but with very incomplete coverage in the first few decades. The individual records are often referred to as *Soldiers' Documents*. They record varying amounts of information, but often include age, place of birth, details of army service, the reason for discharge and a physical description.

Registers of pensions awarded by Chelsea Hospital exist for the whole of the Georgian era, but contain less information than the individual documents. They are in two series, arranged chronologically by date of discharge (WO 116) and by regiment (WO 120), and contain the same information for each soldier. This includes age at discharge, number of years' service and the reason for the award of pension.

Some men who had been born in England but who were serving in Ireland when they were awarded pensions are included in the records of Kilmainham Hospital, the Irish equivalent of Chelsea Hospital, and these records are also held at TNA. Most Chelsea and Kilmainham pension records have now been digitized by Ancestry or Findmypast.

Regimental description books survive for some regiments and usually commence in the nineteenth century. They record age on enlistment and birthplace, as well as physical attributes such as height, complexion, hair colour and eye colour. Army muster rolls survive from the 1760s and enable a soldier's career to be investigated once the regiment is known, although they rarely provide any information about a soldier's origins. Muster rolls record dates of enlistment and discharge, and also the dates of death of men who died in service. Casualty returns have also survived for some regiments. Relatively few records in these categories have been digitized or indexed.

Knowledge of a soldier's regiment is the key to using muster rolls and other sources organized by regiment. The names of regiments are readily available for men who were awarded pensions, but must be established from other sources for men who were not. The names of regiments can sometimes be found in non-military sources such as church registers, but the availability of searchable transcriptions and indexes of selected military records can enable many other men who served in the army to be identified and their regiments to be established. The online records available for this purpose include a collection of Napoleonic War Records on Findmypast, including various indexes produced by Barbara Chambers, and selected muster rolls from 1812 to 1817, which have been digitized by Ancestry.

Medal rolls can provide evidence of army service and an indication of men's regiments, but issuing medals to all the men who served in wars was not normal practice during the Georgian era, and only one medal was issued. All the men who took part in the Battle of Waterloo in 1815 were awarded a medal the following year. The Military General Service Medal (MGSM), sometimes referred to as the Peninsula Medal, was belatedly issued in 1848 to all the men who had served in the wars between 1793 and 1814 and were still alive in 1847. The onus was on men to apply for a medal, and it is likely that some men did not hear about it. Many men had died in the meantime, so only about 26,000 were issued, representing only a fraction of the men who had served in the wars. The MGSM roll lists the campaigns in which men had served, so can provide an outline of their military careers without the need to use muster rolls. It is therefore particular useful in outlining the careers of men who received the medal but had not been awarded pensions. Both sets of medal rolls are held at TNA and can be searched on Ancestry and Findmypast.

Soldiers' wives can be divided into two categories. A limited number of wives were permitted 'on the strength', accompanying their husbands on active service and carrying out paid duties such as washing and cooking. Many soldiers' wives accompanied their husbands 'off the strength'. The presence of soldiers' wives was rarely recorded in army records. Evidence that wives accompanied their husbands may be found in baptism and burial records in areas where men are known to have served.

The wills of soldiers who died overseas were proved at the Prerogative Court of Canterbury. Corporals and sergeants earned more than private soldiers, so were more likely to make wills, and some private soldiers also did so.

Officers

Commissions in the army were usually obtained by purchase, and the relatively low pay of junior officers required either an extremely abstemious lifestyle or a private income. A small number of men were promoted from the ranks during wartime, but most army officers were either younger sons from aristocratic families or had been born into middle-class families, often with a tradition of army service. During the Georgian era commissioned officers entered infantry regiments as ensigns and cavalry regiments as cornets, both equivalent to the rank of second lieutenant. Appointments and promotions of commissioned officers were announced in the *London Gazette*, the archive of which is searchable online. *Army Lists* were published from 1740, arranged by regiment. A complete set is held at TNA, which has been digitized, and various manuscript lists of officers are also available. There was no system of pensions for officers during the Georgian era, but men no longer required or unfit for further service after 1812 could draw half-pay. Officers receiving half-pay were included in army lists. Biographical information about officers may also be available in a wide range of published regimental histories. Sources of this type usually focus on officers' military careers and rarely include genealogical information. This is more likely to be found in non-military sources such as wills, deeds and family papers, birth, death and marriage announcements in newspapers and the *Gentleman's Magazine*, and pedigrees recorded in works such as *Burke's Landed Gentry*.

Service records for some officers have survived, mainly from the early nineteenth century, and relevant records can be identified using the Discovery catalogue. Returns of service for officers on full and half pay in 1828 and 1829, contain genealogical information, and returns for married officers record the name of the spouse, the date of the marriage and the names and dates of birth of any children. These records include returns for older officers on half-pay who had served in the wars with France between 1793 and 1815. The returns for 1829 include officers' dates and places of birth. Information on officers can potentially be found in a range of other sources held at TNA, most of which have not been indexed, and are described in books on researching army ancestors (referred to above).

THE MILITIA

Although militia units had previously been raised for home defence, a new structure of county militia infantry regiments was established in 1757. This 'new' militia was a part-time force that was only 'embodied' when the country was at war and invasion was possible. The militia was therefore embodied for more than half the period between 1757 and 1815. Militiamen trained for twenty-eight days each year in peacetime, but a core of sergeants, corporals and drummers served continuously. Officers were drawn from the local landed gentry, and were often of a higher social status than their army counterparts.

Militiamen were selected by ballot, but had the option to provide a substitute or pay for one to be provided. Because most men who could afford to do so paid for substitutes, most militiamen were from similar social backgrounds to regular soldiers, being mainly labourers and men employed in lower-paid occupations. Unlike soldiers in the regular army, the majority of militiamen were residents of the county in whose regiment they were serving, and most had been born there.

Militia regiments were embodied during wartime and stationed throughout Great Britain, usually outside the counties where they had been raised. They changed location relatively frequently. Most regiments were stationed near the coast and concentrated in areas where invasion was more likely. Some regiments guarded prisoner of war camps, which were usually sited further inland to make escape more difficult. Because the militia could not be sent abroad, serving as a substitute during wartime could be an attractive option for men with limited employment opportunities. Many men transferred from the militia to the regular army, as they received a bounty for doing so. Some militia regiments volunteered for service in Ireland following the Irish Rebellion of 1798.

The Lord Lieutenant of each county was responsible for the militia, so some militia records are held in relevant local archives, often among the Lieutenancy papers, but their survival is very variable. *Militia ballot lists* record all men who were eligible to be included in the ballot, comprising men aged 18–50 before 1762 and 18–45 thereafter, but excluding certain categories such as clergymen and apprentices. These lists are therefore partial census listings, arranged by parish, of the adult male population. There are good collections for some counties, such as Dorset, but few or no lists survive for others. Records usually include names, occupations and infirmities, and after 1802 the number of children aged under and over 14. Transcriptions of some of these lists have been published, and some can be searched online.

Some *militia enrolment lists* are held in local archives. For example, a roll of men who joined the Westmorland Militia on 23 October 1779 at Appleby, is held at Carlisle Archive Centre. It includes men's names, ages, places of birth, occupations, height, complexion, hair colour and eye colour, as well as the parish they were serving for and the person they were serving for. Out of the forty-eight men sworn on that day, only seven were serving as balloted men, thirty-nine were substitutes and two were volunteers.

Muster rolls of the militia when embodied in wartime are held at TNA and are similar to army muster rolls, giving little information about individuals apart from their name and rank, but enabling their locations to be established at specific times. Militia muster rolls generally commence in 1781, and those for 1781 and 1782 have been transcribed and can be searched online on *The Genealogist*. A few muster rolls are held in local archives. The movements of militia regiments were often reported in local newspapers, and some lists of serving militiamen were also published.

The families of married men serving in the embodied militia were able to apply for parish relief under the Poor Law. Payments were made to families by the Overseers of the Poor of the parishes in which the families were living, with reimbursement sought when necessary from the parishes of the balloted men for whom substitutes were serving. Records of payments made to families, and orders for payment, signed by Justices of the Peace, have often survived in parish Poor Law records in local archives.

As well as the county militia regiments, which were fully embodied during wartime, a variety of part-time units were established for local defence, with a similar function to the Home Guard during the Second World War. Many units of volunteer infantry were established in the late 1790s and during the period between 1803 and 1805 when invasion seemed likely. Although the officers were gentry or merchants, the social composition of the other ranks was more variable, and often included men of a higher social status than would have normally joined the army as private soldiers, for example skilled tradesmen, shopkeepers and professional men such as attorneys. Volunteer cavalry were known as Yeomanry or Yeomanry Cavalry, and in rural areas largely consisted of farmers and their sons. A separate local militia was established in 1808. The records of some of these part-time units are now held at TNA, but most surviving records are held in local archives.

Further information on militia records can be found in books on researching army ancestry, but Spencer (1997) provides the most detailed description of the records of the militia and other auxiliary forces. Gibson and Medlycott (2013) lists the surviving militia records for each county, held both locally and nationally.

THE ROYAL NAVY

The Royal Navy became the largest organization in the world during the Georgian era, and the Royal Dockyards were some of the world's largest industrial complexes. First Rate ships of the line, with over 100 guns, such as HMS *Victory*, were the largest moveable man-made objects of their time. They had crews of over 800 men of all social classes and occupations, and resembled small towns.

At the beginning of the Georgian era, ships had to return to port at regular intervals for barnacles and weeds to be removed from their hulls. It was found that sheathing hulls with copper allowed ships to stay at sea for much longer, and all naval warships were coppered from 1780. It was also found that deaths from scurvy on long sea voyages could be virtually eliminated by issuing a daily ration of lemon juice to ships' crews. These two developments enabled ships to stay at sea for much longer and for prolonged blockades to be maintained throughout the Napoleonic War.

Over 90 per cent of naval deaths during wartime were the result of disease, accident or shipwreck. Mosquito-borne diseases, such as malaria and yellow fever, were particularly prevalent in the West Indies. Many sailors regarded a voyage there as a death sentence, and officers tried to avoid this area whenever possible. Naval battles were relatively rare, and when they did occur, were short and intense: the Battle of Trafalgar was over in less than five hours. The aim of naval actions was to disable and capture enemy warships and merchant vessels rather than to sink them. The number of casualties in naval battles was lower than might be expected because it was rare for ships to be sunk. Ships built from oak could sustain enemy fire for many hours and still remain afloat. They usually sank only if their powder magazines exploded, and no British ships were sunk as a result of enemy action between 1793 and 1815.

Unlike the army, in which there was a sharp dividing line between officers and other ranks, the naval hierarchy included the intermediate level of warrant officer. Warrant officers included the master, boatswain, carpenter, gunner and purser. There were also inferior officers such as the ship's cook. Ships were complex machines requiring a combination of specific skills, and although social class was still important, a substantial minority of naval officers rose from relatively humble origins. In contrast to the army, the career structure of the Georgian navy was more like a ladder, which it was possible for talented individuals to ascend. There were, however, two significant barriers to progress. A good level of education was required to become a warrant officer, and the ability to conduct oneself as a gentleman was necessary to become a commissioned officer. Although talented but uneducated men might become very competent able seamen, they were unlikely to progress further.

The extent of surviving naval records is vast, and only a small proportion have been digitized or indexed. Using the full range of sources in which information might potentially be found requires either spending time at TNA and becoming familiar with the records or employing a specialist researcher. Further information on researching naval ancestors can be found in Rodger (1988), Pappalardo (2003), Fowler (2011) and Waller (2014).

Ratings

Continuous service for naval ratings was only introduced in the mid-nineteenth century, so there are no naval service records for the Georgian era. Warships needed large crews for fighting battles, but these were infrequent and of short duration, so for most of the time life on warships was easier than on merchant vessels, although the pay was much lower. The Royal Navy required large numbers of experienced seamen during wartime. It is commonly believed that press gangs dragged young men who had never been to sea away from their homes. Such incidents did occur, but the purpose of press gangs was to impress experienced seamen. Taverns in coastal towns frequented by seamen were targeted, and merchant ships returning to port were intercepted. Aboard HMS *Victory* at the Battle of Trafalgar, 289 seamen were volunteers and 217 had been pressed.

Naval ratings are listed in ships' musters and pay books, but few have been indexed by name, so using them requires the name of the ship to be known. However, some musters and pay books have now been digitized by Findmypast, which may enable records for some individuals to be identified. Unlike army musters, which record only names, the forms used after 1761 included provision for recording place of birth and age, although this was not always done. Deaths and desertions were recorded in muster rolls. Although crews sometimes followed popular captains, tracing men's naval careers from ship to ship using unindexed muster rolls may not always be possible, particularly if service in the Royal Navy was interspersed with periods in the merchant service.

Each county was required to raise a certain number of men under the Navy Quota Acts of 1795 and 1796. Justices of the Peace set the quota for

HMS Victory. First Rates such as her had crews of over 800 men. Crews were listed in muster rolls, which are now held at TNA.

each parish and a bounty was paid to men enlisting. When there were insufficient volunteers, men convicted of petty crimes were given the option to join the navy as an alternative to imprisonment. Returns were sent by parishes to the Clerk of the Peace listing names, ages, places of birth or settlement and occupations. Many of these records have survived in Quarter Sessions records in local archives. A few returns are held at TNA, such as those for the port of London and the Isle of Wight.

Allotment registers from 1795 to 1812 and from 1830 to 1852 in series ADM 27 at TNA record the allotment of part of a rating's pay to a dependant, usually a wife or mother. The information recorded included the name of the ship, the name of the person to whom the allotment was to be paid, their address, their relationship to the rating, the number of children and the pay-office where the money was to be collected. These records have been digitized and can be searched on Findmypast.

There is a one in six chance that a man serving in the Royal Navy in 1805 took part in the Battle of Trafalgar. There are two online listings of the men who served at Trafalgar, which include the names of their ships: the *Ayshford Trafalgar Roll* and TNA's *Trafalgar Ancestors*. They were produced from the muster rolls of the ships that were present. No general service medals were issued during the Georgian era. The Naval General Service Medal (NGSM), based on service in selected actions between 1793 and 1840, was belatedly issued to men who were still alive in 1847, but only about 21,000 were given out. As with the medal issued to soldiers the same year, this represented only a fraction of the men who had served. The NGSM roll is held at TNA and can be searched on Ancestry.

Before 1804 pensions to disabled seamen, both in-pensions to residents of Greenwich Hospital and out-pensions to men living independently, were paid out of the Chatham Chest, but subsequently they were paid by Greenwich Hospital, so men in receipt of pensions were known as Greenwich Pensioners. Several different record series relating to naval pensions are held at TNA, and they have been digitized by Findmypast. There are often several records for each man, containing varying amounts of information. The more detailed records include age, whether married, number of children, place of birth, last place of residence, occupation, ship's name and details of wounds.

Ships often remained at sea for several months, so when ratings died in service, even though they might have owned virtually nothing, they would often have accumulated substantial arrears of pay. Ratings were therefore encouraged to make wills on printed forms before sailing. Most of these wills were very brief, giving only the rank, the name of the ship, and the name, and sometimes the address, of the person nominated to receive the effects, usually the next of kin. Some wills were proved at the Prerogative Court of Canterbury, which also issued letters of administration to the next of kin of some men who had died without making wills. A further collection of wills of ratings and warrant officers from 1786 is held at TNA in series ADM 48. This series has been digitized and the records can be searched using the Discovery catalogue.

Officers

Naval officers were divided into warrant officers and commissioned officers, and both were included in the *Navy List,* published from 1782. No systematic service records for either were kept during the Georgian era.

Most commissioned officers were from middle- and upper-class backgrounds and began their naval careers as midshipmen at the age of 12 or 13. Having learned the skills of seamanship and navigation, they then took lieutenancy examinations. The naval rank of lieutenant was higher than the army rank of the same name, and was equivalent to a captain or major. Lieutenants' passing certificates are held at TNA and often record age and place of birth. After 1779 they are sometimes accompanied by copies of baptism certificates. Passing certificates are not listed individually in the Discovery catalogue, but there is a published index available (Pappalardo, 2001).

The man in charge of a warship in the Georgian era was usually referred to as its 'commander'. Smaller ships were commanded by lieutenants. The description 'captain' was used to refer to the naval rank of captain, sometimes referred to as 'post captain', which was equivalent in status to the army rank of lieutenant colonel. The master of a ship in the Royal Navy was a warrant officer responsible for navigation. Lieutenants in charge of ships were expected to act as their own masters, so the description 'Master and Commander' may be found in late eighteenth-century records.

Because commissioned officers were usually from middle- and upper-class backgrounds, genealogical information can often be found in non-military sources, such as wills and published sources. Further information on officers can potentially be found in a range of other sources held at TNA, which are described in books on researching naval ancestry (referred to above).

THE ROYAL MARINES

The Marines were permanently established in 1755, although maritime regiments had been formed and then disbanded during earlier periods. In 1802, when their numbers had reached 30,000, the Marines became the Royal Marines. They served on board ship, both as a military unit and to protect the officers from the crew. During naval battles they raked enemy ships with musket fire and engaged the enemy at close quarters. Marines also took part in amphibious landings, and acted as dockyard guards during peacetime, but this role was taken over by the militia during wartime.

The Marines were organized into three divisions, based at Plymouth, Portsmouth and Chatham, and all were volunteers. Attestation and discharge forms from 1790 are held at TNA in series ADM 157. These are listed individually in the Discovery catalogue, and include birthplace and age at enlistment. Description books from 1750 in series ADM 158 also include birthplace and age at enlistment. They summarize information in attestation forms, but may cover periods for which attestation and discharge forms no longer survive. Wills and pension records relating to Royal Marines may be found in the same sources as the records relating to Royal Navy ratings. Officers in the Royal Marines were listed in the *Navy List*. As with naval officers, there is no single source, and further information may be found in a range of sources at TNA. The sources available for tracing Royal Marines are described in Brooks and Little (2008) and Divall (2008).

THE ROYAL DOCKYARDS

The Royal Dockyards were situated in Plymouth, Portsmouth, Sheerness, Chatham, Deptford and Woolwich, and all grew into major industrial complexes during the Georgian era. A large collection of yard pay-lists is held at TNA. These records contain no genealogical information, but include start and end dates and sometimes pension information. Like ships' muster rolls they are unindexed, so using them is dependent on finding a clue in another source that a man was employed in a naval dockyard.

A volunteer project is listing a collection of Navy Board records held at TNA and the Library of the National Maritime Museum at Greenwich. These records include many lists of employees and letters concerning them. The information recorded about individuals includes transfers between yards, deaths in service and applications for superannuation. Many records relating to individuals are now included in the Discovery catalogue. The identification of dockyard employees in these records can enable further research in pay-lists to be carried out.

Chapter 8

SOCIAL STATUS AND PROSPERITY

Understanding the position of ancestors in the social hierarchy does not just provide an insight into what their daily lives might have been like. It can also facilitate selection of the most appropriate sources for research, and enable the information in sources to be correctly interpreted. For example, it is virtually inconceivable that the recipient of a legacy of £1,000 in Georgian England could have been an agricultural labourer.

The social hierarchy that existed during the Georgian era is discussed in this chapter, together with indications of social status that may be found in records, such as titles and sums of money. Sources that are particularly relevant to more prosperous ancestors, such as pedigrees, family histories, recorded memorial inscriptions and freemasonry records, are also discussed.

SOCIAL STATUS

All children in England today, whatever their parents' background, have educational opportunities that enable them to develop their abilities and ultimately realize their potential, at least in theory. Such opportunities did not exist during the Georgian era, when most people remained in the social class into which they had been born, irrespective of their abilities or talents. The dependence of social status on the circumstances of birth was accepted as normal in the Georgian era, even by many people at the lower end of the social hierarchy, who had been taught that to seek to rise above their station in life was a sin. William Wilberforce (1759–1833), a vigorous

121

campaigner against slavery and a social reformer, nevertheless said of the poor that 'their more lowly path has been allotted to them by the hand of God: that it is their part faithfully to discharge its duties and contentedly to bear its inconveniences'.

People in Georgian England also had quite a different view of what today would be regarded as corruption, and personal influence and patronage was accepted as a normal part of life. Advancement and promotion were often dependent on knowing someone in a position of influence, and the relatively few people from humble backgrounds who ascended the social hierarchy often did so as a result of sponsorship by a more prosperous patron.

Because most people remained in the class into which they had been born, social status usually remained constant from generation to generation. Although prosperity increased in a continuum from the very poor to the extremely rich, for the purposes of genealogical research it is convenient to divide the population into three major categories: the upper, middle and lower classes.

The *upper class* were the landed elite, consisting of the aristocracy and major gentry, who essentially governed the country. The power of the monarch had been curtailed by the Bill of Rights of 1689, and Parliament, comprising the House of Lords and the House of Commons, consisted almost entirely of landowners. At the local level, before elected county councils were established towards the end of the Victorian era, counties were also governed by landowners, who occupied the positions of Lord Lieutenant and Justice of the Peace. The landed class derived their income from rents paid by tenants, which gradually increased during the Georgian era as the value of land increased. The countryside of Georgian England became dominated by large estates, landscaped gardens and stately homes, often built during wartime when many lower-class families were suffering from food shortages and high prices. The increasing prosperity of the upper class during the Georgian era led to a large expansion of the country sports of hunting and shooting. The right to take game was dependent on the ownership of land of a certain value, so in practice was restricted to the upper class. They employed gamekeepers to breed and preserve pheasants and partridges at the same time as the lower class were being deprived of their access to common land through enclosure.

The landed class made up only a very small proportion of the population, so relatively few readers are likely to have upper-class ancestry, which was the traditional focus of genealogy in the past and has therefore been extensively documented in works such as *Burke's Peerage* and *Burke's Landed Gentry*. Further information on researching ancestors from this background can be found in Adolph (2013) and Raymond (2012a). However, many people lower down the social scale were employed by landowning families or rented land from them, so the records of landed estates, often now deposited in public archives but sometimes still held by the families themselves, can be a rich source of family history information.

The *middle class* comprised people from a wide variety of backgrounds who did not engage in manual labour, were reasonably prosperous, and could usually read and write. They included Anglican

Castle Howard in Yorkshire, the seat of the Earls of Carlisle. Very few people have ancestors who owned such properties, but many more have ancestors who worked in them.

clergymen, lawyers, officers in the army and navy, physicians, surgeons, apothecaries, merchants, master craftsmen, minor country gentlemen, yeoman farmers and larger tenant farmers. People from the middle class shared certain characteristics that are relevant to the sources in which they are likely to be found. Because children usually learned to read and write, their signatures as adults may appear in sources such as marriage records, wills and deeds. Orphaned children were usually provided for and brought up by guardians. Middle-class couples were usually from similar social backgrounds and often married by licence, which was more expensive but more discreet, as it did not require the public reading of banns. Middle-class people often owned land, sometimes in more than one county, for which there may be surviving deeds, and paid church and poor rates and Land Tax. They also rented private pews in churches. They frequently left wills, and if they died intestate it was usually necessary for their next of kin to apply for letters of administration. After death they were often commemorated by memorial inscriptions in churches and churchyards. During the later Georgian period their births, marriages and deaths were often reported in newspapers and other publications such as the *Gentleman's Magazine*. People from middle-class backgrounds engaged in civil disputes over land, property and inheritance in the equity courts more frequently than might be expected, so Chancery Proceedings can be a rich source of genealogical information.

The middle class could afford to keep horses and use horse-drawn transport, and were more likely to travel, for both business and pleasure. Aspirational individuals and families participated in similar leisure activities to the upper class, visiting the spa towns of Bath, Harrogate, Leamington Spa and Cheltenham and the seaside resorts of Weymouth and Brighton. The novels of Jane Austen, written during the Regency period, depict individuals and families from the middle and upper classes. Although the historical background of novels set during the Georgian era is often substantially accurate, novelists may have stretched credibility to its limits for the sake of a good story. Historical novels may portray 'gentlemen' marrying their servants, who are subsequently transformed into 'ladies', which although not impossible, would have been very unlikely. Men from the middle and upper classes did have relationships with lower-class women, and fathered children by them, which they often subsequently acknowledged and provided for, but marriage between two people of such different social status was very rare.

The *lower class* consisted of skilled tradesmen such as tailors, carpenters, blacksmiths, butchers, bakers and shoemakers, and unskilled and semi-skilled workers such as industrial and agricultural labourers, servants, soldiers and sailors, and increasing numbers of mill and other factory workers in the second half of the Georgian era. Levels of literacy varied. Newspapers were relatively expensive and subject to Stamp Duty throughout the Georgian era. A typical newspaper in the early nineteenth century cost sixpence (2.5p) at a time when many lower-paid workers earned only a shilling (5p) a day. Few lower-class families could afford to buy newspapers, but they were sometimes shared and read aloud, particularly in public houses. Birth, death and marriage notices relating to lower-class families rarely appeared in newspapers until well into the Victorian era.

Although skilled tradesmen were somewhat more prosperous than unskilled labourers, the illness or death of a significant breadwinner could result in a considerable reduction in a family's standard of living. The Poor Law, when administered as intended, provided basic subsistence for individuals and families who fell on hard times, but this sometimes involved being removed to another parish (as discussed in the next chapter). Orphans and other poor children were often bound as parish apprentices, sometimes being sent away from their home parish.

People from lower-class families usually married after banns, which was the cheaper alternative, but soldiers and sailors, who sometimes received bounties or large payments of wages in arrears, and for whom the calling of banns was often impracticable, were more likely to marry by licence.

Most travel was on foot, so many people did not travel very far from their homes. Travel further afield was usually in connection with employment, and those who travelled significant distances included soldiers, sailors and men employed in the transport of goods, animals

BIRTHS.] On Saturday, in New Norfolk-street, the Lady of John Hammet, Esq. M. P. of a son.—A few days since, at Ridgeway, near Plympton, the Lady of Capt. Pym, of the Royal Navy, of a son and heir.

MARRIED.] On Monday. at Bristol, Captain Elton, eldest son of the Rev. Sir Abraham Elton, Bart. to Miss Smith, daughter of Joseph Smith, Esq. merchant, of Bristol.—Same day, at St. Margaret's, Westminster, J. Elliot, Esq. brewer, of Milbank, Colonel of the West-minster Cavalry, to Miss Lettsom, of Grove Hill, Camberwell, daughter of the late Dr. Lettsom.—On Tuesday, at Marybone Church, Capt. Graham, of the 15th Light Dragoons, to Miss Maria Cooke, youngest daughter of the late G. J. Cooke, Esq. of Harefield.

DIED.] On Friday last, at Port Eliot, Cornwall, seven days after the death of her late Lord, the Right Hon. Lady Eliot, aged 69 years.—On Friday evening, at his Lordship's house in Grosvenor-place, the Right Hon. Ann Countess of Ossory ; her Ladyship was the only daughter of the late Lord Ravensworth, and was first married to the Duke of Grafton, by whom she was the mother of the present Earl of Euston, of Lord Charles Fitzroy, and of Lady Georgiana Smith : this marriage was dissolved by Act of Parliament on the 23d of March 1769, and on the 26th she was married to Lord Ossory, by whom she has left two daughters. —On Saturday, at Grenier's Hotel, Albemarle-street, Ralph Dutton, Esq. brother to Lord Sherborne. —On Monday, the Lady of Drummond Smith, Esq. at his house at Hyde-park Corner.—On the 19th of January, at North Berwick, Col. Geo Dalrymple, of the 19th regiment of foot.—On the 23d inst. at his seat near Plymouth, aged 70 years, John Culme, Esq. of Tothill, a truly respectable old English gentleman.—On the 15th inst. at Edinburgh, Dr. Thomas Gillespie —Yesterday, at his house in Bridge-street, Blackfriars, John Horrocks, Esq. M. P. for Preston, in Lancashire.—Lately, at Litton, near Wells, Samuel Curtis, aged 107 years.—A few days ago, Mrs. Day, of Thurmaston, Leicestershire, aged 82 ; she was sitting alone by the fire, a spark set a part of her dress in a blaze, and burnt her so dreadfully as to occasion her death.—On Friday se'nnight, a poor woman of Cardiff, aged 105 years : in her way from Cardiff to Newport, she fell into a gravel-pit, in which was a small quantity of water, and was drowned.

Births, marriages and deaths reported in an issue of the Salisbury and Winchester Journal *from 1804. The majority relate to people from the middle and upper classes, but newsworthy reports relating to people from further down the social scale are also included, such as people living to a great age or dying in unusual circumstances.*

or people. Servants employed by upper-class families sometimes moved between their employers' estates.

The lower class were prohibited by the game laws from trapping and killing game, so some men became poachers, and others were employed as gamekeepers.

People belonging to the lower class rarely owned land, but some leased small acreages. Few people from the lower class left wills, but a small proportion did. One sibling sometimes became significantly more prosperous than the others, through hard work or good fortune. Lower-class families could rarely afford to pay for gravestones, and those that were erected were relatively small.

Significant changes in social status from one generation to the next rarely occurred during the Georgian era, but prosperity could vary from generation to generation, between siblings, and across an individual's lifetime, often as a result of unpredictable events. These might include the death of a significant breadwinner, an unexpected inheritance, or social changes, such as those resulting from the introduction of new machines or the enclosure of land.

Surnames evolved during the Middle Ages, and by the Georgian era it was not uncommon for unrelated families with the same surname, though of different levels of social status, to have coexisted in the same parish for many generations. Novice researchers often assume that everyone living in a parish with the same surname must have been related, and some fanciful family stories may have arisen in the past because previous generations made similar assumptions.

Although occupation can provide an indication of prosperity, it may be difficult or impossible to establish, particularly in the eighteenth century. Nevertheless, it may still be possible to infer people's relative prosperity from the records of the period, even in the absence of occupational information. Clues to relative prosperity include the presence or absence of titles such as Mr, Mrs and Esquire, and the amounts of money people were paid or paid to others.

Titles

The significance of the title *Mr*, originally short for 'Master', gradually changed during the Georgian era. In the early eighteenth century, a man would only be referred to as 'Mr John Smith' if he was in a position of authority over others, such as servants, employees, apprentices or pupils. By the early nineteenth century, Mr was evolving into a title for all adult males, and Master a form of address for boys and young men. During most of the Georgian era, therefore, the appearance in records of a man's name prefixed by Mr denotes a man of higher social status who was reasonably prosperous, such as a merchant, gentleman farmer or yeoman farmer, but below the rank of 'Esquire' (discussed below).

'Mrs' was the female equivalent of Mr, and was short for 'Mistress', signifying a woman who had authority over others, such as servants, employees, apprentices or pupils. It was not originally an indication of marital status. The description of a woman as 'Mrs Mary Smith' in records of the early eighteenth century does not imply that she was or had been married, but that she was a woman of higher social status. By the nineteenth century Mrs was evolving into a title for married women, although it continued to be used for unmarried women of higher social status. Miss was also an abbreviation of Mistress. It was originally used for young girls in families of higher social status, and changed to Mrs on reaching adulthood. The changes in meaning over time of the descriptions 'Mrs' and 'Miss' are explained in Erickson (2012).

Society in the Middle Ages had been very hierarchical, and although social distinctions gradually became less rigid, the same categories persisted throughout the Georgian era, and in rural areas comprised the following:

Esquires
Gentlemen
Yeomen
Husbandmen
Labourers

The title *Esquire*, written after the name, as in 'John Smith, Esquire', and usually abbreviated to 'John Smith, Esq.' denoted a man from the untitled landed gentry, who was often Lord of the Manor. It was also accorded to men by virtue of their occupational status, such as barristers and Justices of the Peace.

A *gentleman* was originally a landowner between the rank of Esquire and yeoman, but the definition became more fluid during the Georgian era, when being a gentleman also implied refinement and certain standards of behaviour. Country gentlemen might concede that a merchant conducted himself as a gentleman in business matters, but would not consider him to be a gentleman like themselves, even if he were considerably more prosperous. To become a gentleman in their eyes required buying a country estate and leaving the 'taint of trade' behind. It might only be his son or grandson who would finally be accepted as a country gentleman. The change in the meaning of gentleman that took place during the Georgian era was related to the expansion of the middle class, as a result of an increase in trade and the Industrial Revolution. By the nineteenth century, men were beginning to be defined by their occupation rather than their social origins, and the term gentleman evolved to refer to a man who had inherited or earned sufficient capital so that he no longer needed to work. The definition of a gentleman therefore now embraced men from humble backgrounds who had subsequently prospered.

A name recorded as 'William Brown, gent.' indicates only that the person making the record considered the man concerned to be a gentleman. Not only did the meaning of gentleman gradually change over time, but its interpretation varied widely between rural and urban areas and from parish to parish. Despite this considerable variation, the description 'gent.' implies a man of some prosperity. A man who was considered to be a gentleman would be addressed as Mr, but not all men addressed as Mr would be considered to be gentlemen.

A *yeoman* was a farmer who owned his own land and usually employed farm servants or agricultural labourers. A *husbandman* was a tenant farmer.

Although titles such as Esquire, gentleman and Mr were neither precisely defined nor consistently used in the records of the period, they can provide an important indication of social status, enabling families living in the same area with the same surname to be differentiated. For example, in a list of parish inhabitants paying the poor rate, it was normal practice to list ratepayers in descending order of social status, which was dependent on the amount of land they owned and therefore the amount of tax they paid. At the head of the list would be the Lord of the Manor, with the title Esq. after his name, followed by gentlemen and then yeoman farmers whose names were prefixed with the title Mr. Next would come men listed under only their names, such as husbandmen and tradesmen. Men who were not listed at all were too poor to pay rates, but were not necessarily so poor that they received parish relief. The majority of able-bodied and employed labourers are likely to have fallen into this category.

Monetary Values

English currency developed in Anglo-Saxon times and remained substantially the same until decimalization in 1971. Older readers will have had direct experience of shillings and pence, and some may remember farthings, withdrawn from circulation in 1960. Younger readers have no direct experience of the 'old money' or how sums of money were written down, so a brief summary will be given here.

A pound consisted of twenty shillings, each consisting of twelve pence. The symbols for shillings and pence were 's' and 'd', from the Latin *solidus* and *denarius*. Fractions of a penny were the halfpenny, or ha'penny and the farthing, represented as ½d and ¼d. A sum in pounds, shillings and pence was written as £1-9-6½ or £1-9-6½d or £1-9s-6½d, denoting one pound nine shillings and sixpence ha'penny. A sum in shillings and pence was written in the form 9s 6½d or 9/6½d, denoting nine shillings and sixpence ha'penny. A sum in pence was written in the form 6½d, denoting sixpence ha'penny. A guinea was one pound one shilling, £1-1s-0d. As an example of conversion between pre-decimal and decimal currency, thirteen shillings and sixpence, 13s 6d, was equivalent to 67.5p, but was obviously worth a lot more than that at the time, representing more than a week's wages for many lower-paid workers.

The average annual rate of inflation from 1714 to 1837 was 0.5 per cent, so £100 in 1714 was equivalent to only £175 in 1837. Prices

A penny and a shilling from the reign of George III. A shilling was a twentieth of a pound, and consisted of twelve pence. Weekly wages during the Georgian era were measured in shillings.

gradually rose in the second half of the eighteenth century, increased sharply during the French Revolutionary and Napoleonic Wars, and then gradually fell. Such a low average rate of inflation over such a long period of time means that although prices and wages fluctuated, sums of money recorded in historical documents throughout the Georgian era were of comparable orders of magnitude.

Weekly wages were measured in shillings, with labourers often earning less than ten shillings (50p) a week, or £25 a year. This is in sharp contrast to members of the middle and upper classes. In Jane Austen's *Pride and Prejudice*, for example, published in 1813, Mr Bennet has an income of £2,000 per year, or £40 per week. He is married to the daughter of an attorney, and in economic terms can be regarded as middle class, but socially he is a member of the minor landed gentry. The eligible Mr Darcy, from a gentry family with aristocratic connections, has an income of £10,000 a year, or £200 per week.

Inheritance

Apart from its relevance to royal and aristocratic lines of succession the concept of the *heir* has largely died out. Although most people today would consider it unfair for parents to favour one of their children without a very good reason, heirship was of some significance to the larger families of the Georgian era, particularly middle- and upper-class families that owned land. There is a distinction in law between *real property,* consisting of land and buildings and *personal property,* consisting of goods and chattels. During the Georgian era real property was often inherited according to the principle of *primogeniture,* meaning inheritance by the eldest son as heir. The principle of primogeniture applied both as a practice and as a legal concept.

As a practice, primogeniture involved freehold land being held in *fee tail,* whereby it could not be sold but only inherited by an heir, who was usually the eldest son. Such a restriction was made binding by means of a legal device known as an *entail.* Land was sometimes entailed in *tail male,* meaning that it could only be inherited by the closest male heir, who was sometimes quite a distant relative.

The legal concept of primogeniture applied when a man died intestate. His eldest son automatically inherited all his real property, and the younger children, and even the widow, inherited none. If there were no sons, the real property was divided equally among the daughters, who were known as *co-heirs.*

Although the principle of primogeniture dominated during the Georgian era, it was not universal. Owners who held land in *fee simple* could dispose of it as they wished, both within their own lifetimes and in their wills. Manorial land was inherited according to the customs of individual manors. Inheritance in most manors was by primogeniture, but land in some manors was inherited by the youngest son, a practice known as *ultimogeniture* or *Borough English.* A third system of inheritance, particularly in Kent, was *partible inheritance* or *gavelkind,* by which land was divided among all sons equally.

In upper- and middle-class families, financial provision was made for a woman after the death of her husband by her father providing land or money at the time of the marriage. This was held in trust and its future use specified in a legal document known as a *marriage settlement*. Unmarried women and widows could own both real and personal property and make wills, but the situation was quite different for married women. On marriage a woman's property was transferred to the ownership of her husband and she was unable to make a will without his consent. However, a married woman could receive and inherit property if it was specified as being for her own personal use in legal documents such as wills, prenuptial agreements and marriage settlements.

Primogeniture, entails and marriage settlements, combined with unpredictable life events such as the death of a childless heir or all surviving children being daughters, could have a significant and sometimes sudden effect on the prosperity of individuals and families. The vicissitudes of inheritance applied not only to the upper class, but also to the middle class and some tradesmen, and were relevant to businesses as well as land. Younger sons from upper-class families generally had to make their own way in life by entering professions such as the church, army or navy, but their prospects of advancement were often enhanced by family connections. It was normal practice for the eldest son of a yeoman farmer to take over the farm after his father's death, so younger sons might be apprenticed to trades, become tenant farmers, or in some cases end up as agricultural labourers. All the sons of a blacksmith in a small village might learn the trade from their father, but with the expectation that the eldest son would carry on the business and one or more younger sons would have to seek work elsewhere.

Entails and marriage settlements appear as themes in novels such as *Pride and Prejudice*. Mr Bennet's land is entailed in tail male, he has no sons but five daughters, so when he dies the land will automatically pass to a distant male relative, Mr Collins. Mr Bennet's land brings him an income of £2,000 per year, but after his death Mrs Bennet's income will be reduced to £200 per year, derived from four per cent interest on her £5,000 marriage settlement. However, that would still have left her in a relatively comfortable position compared to an agricultural labourer earning a tenth of that amount and with a large family to support.

Younger sons of younger sons could gradually slip down the social scale as a result of the operation of primogeniture in successive generations, so it is not uncommon for an industrial or agricultural labourer in the nineteenth century to have had significantly more prosperous ancestors living a century earlier. The fall in the standard of living among all but the richest after 1815 seems to have pushed many people even further down the social scale.

Inheritance also affected the very poorest members of society who sought relief under the Poor Law. As discussed in the next chapter, women took their husband's settlement on marriage, and people who had not obtained settlements of their own inherited the settlement of their father. A poor widow could therefore inherit a settlement from her late husband's father, or even his grandfather, and potentially be removed to a parish where she had never lived, which could be hundreds of miles away.

PEDIGREES AND FAMILY HISTORIES

Genealogy in the traditional sense involved the compilation of pedigrees, and most genealogical research before the Second World War was concerned with middle- and upper-class families. The information in works such as *Burke's Landed Gentry* was supplied by the families themselves. Other pedigrees can be found in volumes of published pedigrees, family histories, county histories and local histories. Many of these pedigrees have been listed in Marshall (1903), Whitmore (1953) and Barrow (1977), which can often be found in larger libraries. Digitized versions of Marshall are available online.

The College of Arms was established in 1484 to regulate and register coats of arms and pedigrees, so a close relationship developed between heraldry and genealogy. A large collection of genealogical material is now held at the College in London, which is not directly accessible to members of the public, although a paid research service is available. Coats of arms belong to specific individuals and are inherited according to certain rules, so there is no such thing as a coat of arms for a surname. Genealogical relationships are depicted by combining coats of arms together, again according to certain rules. During the sixteenth and seventeenth centuries, the Heralds of the College of Arms travelled around the country at intervals to ensure that coats of arms were only used by those having the right to do so. This involved the recording of pedigrees, which were of varying degrees of accuracy, depending on the extent to which individual Heralds required proof of the information presented to them. The College of Arms entered a period of decline during the Georgian era, when no visitations were carried out. Some men, particularly those who had become prosperous through trade and wished to accelerate their transformation into 'gentlemen', compiled erroneous pedigrees, either deliberately or unwittingly, and adopted coats of arms without either having the right to do so or applying for new grants of arms.

Recorded pedigrees should not be assumed to be correct just because they are old. They need to be supported by documentary evidence. However, pedigrees can often provide a useful starting point, and may contain valuable clues, enabling the information they contain to be either verified or disproved using other sources such as wills, deeds and Chancery Proceedings.

CHANGES OF SURNAME

Childless landowners sometimes left their estates to more distant relatives on condition they adopt their surnames. Edward Austen, Jane Austen's brother, changed his surname to Knight when he inherited the Chawton estate belonging to his father's cousin Thomas Knight. Thomas Knight's father had changed his surname twice. He had been baptized as Thomas Brodnax, changed his surname to May after inheriting an earlier estate and again to Knight after inheriting Chawton. In *Pride and Prejudice* the fact that Mr Collins will inherit Mr Bennet's property in tail male implies that they are both descended from a common ancestor through the male line. Their different surnames are an indication of at least one previous change of surname, most probably on receiving an inheritance. Jane Austen did not specify their relationship; nor did she consider it necessary to explain the reason for such an apparent incongruity, which would have appeared unremarkable to people from her social background at that time.

Changes of surname were often associated with transfers of coats of arms, for which a Royal Licence was necessary. Some records relating to change of surname are held at TNA and the College of Arms, but they are not searchable online. This practice was largely restricted to the landed gentry, so such changes of surname are often recorded in pedigrees and works such as *Burke's Landed Gentry*.

MEMORIAL INSCRIPTIONS

During the Georgian era, tablets inside churches and the majority of gravestones in churchyards were erected by middle- and upper-class families, but some simple gravestones were erected by more prosperous lower-class families. It was common practice for members of the same family to be buried in the same grave, so inscriptions for several family members were often recorded on the same gravestone. Memorial inscriptions can sometimes provide the key to overcoming brick walls. Genealogical information and clues that may be found in memorial inscriptions include age at death, which was rarely recorded in parish registers before 1813, relationships between family members, occupations, and occasionally references to place of birth or usual place of abode.

Many gravestones from the Georgian era no longer survive, and the inscriptions on those that do are often illegible or only partly legible. Memorial inscriptions for members of the gentry and prosperous merchants are more likely to be found inside churches than in churchyards. Wall tablets inside churches are protected from the weather and their inscriptions may still be legible after several centuries. Inscriptions on floor slabs may have been worn away by foot traffic or covered over. The legibility of gravestones in churchyards is dependent on factors such as their location, the local climate, the amount of air pollution and the type of stone used. The recording of memorial inscriptions increased after the 1960s when local family history societies started to be established. Inscriptions recorded half a century ago can be very valuable today, as many of the stones have been further eroded and some may now be entirely illegible. Only one or two copies may have been made of inscriptions recorded towards the end of the twentieth century. They are usually now held in archives, local studies libraries, the research centres of local family history societies, or the Society of Genealogists.

Memorial inscriptions in some churches and churchyards were recorded much earlier, and may contain genealogical information that is now difficult or impossible to establish from other sources. Volumes of inscriptions have been published for some areas. Older published volumes that are out of copyright have often been digitized and are available online through Google Books or the Internet Archive.

RYMER (266).   Here lieth the body of Mr. RICHARD RYMER, of the Parish of Greenwich, Joiner, who departed this life 21 July, 1760, aged 55 years.

Also Mrs. SARAH HUGHES, daughter of the above Richard Rymer, who died the 19 August, 1763, aged 27 years.

Also ANN HUGHES, her daughter, who died the 25 August, 1763, aged 2 months.

Also ELEANOR RYMER, wife of the above, who departed this life 2 April, 1765, aged 66 years.

A memorial inscription from the parish churchyard at Charlton in Kent (now in the London Borough of Greenwich) recorded in a volume published in 1908.

Some unpublished manuscript collections of inscriptions are held in libraries and archives. For example, a collection of inscriptions for 128 parishes in north Devon, recorded between 1769 and 1793, is held at North Devon Record Office in Barnstaple.

Memorial inscriptions that no longer survive may have been recorded in county and local histories published during the Georgian era or shortly afterwards. *The History and Antiquities of the County of Northampton,* by George Baker, published in 1822, for example, includes many inscriptions for people who died in the eighteenth century.

FREEMASONRY

Freemasonry is a fraternal order with its roots in the Middle Ages. Membership of masonic lodges increased dramatically during the Georgian era, particularly among men engaged in skilled occupations and professions. A Masonic Grand Lodge was established in 1717, merging with another lodge to form the United Grand Lodge of England in 1813. Membership records from 1751 are held at the Library and Museum of Freemasonry in London and have been digitized by Ancestry. These records include members of lodges throughout England and although they do not include genealogical information, many records include details of age, abode and occupation. A few historical records are still held by lodges, and others have been deposited in local archives. Lodges were required to submit lists of members to the Clerk of the Peace after 1799, and these lists can often be found in Quarter Sessions records in local archives. Further information on researching ancestors who were freemasons can be found in Lewis (2012).

Chapter 9

POVERTY

Poor Law records have the potential to provide a great deal of information about the lives of poorer ancestors: not only those families who were afflicted by endemic poverty, but also people who unexpectedly fell on hard times. Records may include details of genealogical relationships that would be difficult or impossible to establish from other sources. Poor Law records can also provide evidence that more prosperous ancestors owned or occupied property of sufficient value to pay poor rates or act as Churchwardens or Overseers of the Poor.

Unlike parish registers and wills, Poor Law records were not routinely preserved, so their survival is very variable. However, those Poor Law records that have survived can often enable brick walls to be overcome. Identifying Poor Law records requires knowledge of the various archival collections in which they are likely to be found and the search tools that may be available. Interpreting their contents requires an understanding of how the Poor Law operated.

THE POOR LAW

People are often surprised to learn that a form of 'welfare state' existed in England from the beginning of the seventeenth century. That this is not more widely understood is largely the consequence of significant changes to the Poor Law that occurred in 1834, which resulted in the introduction of the prison-like workhouses portrayed in the novels of Charles Dickens and other Victorian writers. In the late eighteenth and early nineteenth centuries the expenditure on poor relief had increased dramatically during a period of almost constant war, rapid economic and social change and increasing population. Early political economists deliberated on the problems of poverty and population increase, and Thomas Robert Malthus concluded that early marriage, and therefore population growth, was encouraged by supporting the able-bodied poor. Many members of the ruling class came to the conclusion that the only solution was to discourage such people from applying for poor relief. A Royal Commission set up in 1832 proposed that poor relief for those capable of work should only be offered in workhouses in which the conditions of life were more basic than those of the poorest working labourer. The Poor Law Amendment Act of 1834 grouped parishes into Poor Law Unions, which were required to establish workhouses. Although some workhouses had been set up earlier, they were relatively rare. After 1834, many poor families preferred to live in relative destitution than to enter workhouses where families were split up. The descriptions *Old Poor Law* and *New Poor Law* are used to refer to the periods before and after the 1834 Act. The provisions of the Act were implemented only gradually, particularly in the north of England, so the New Poor Law is not discussed further in this book.

The Poor Relief Act of 1601 made parishes responsible for poor relief, and a further act of 1662, commonly referred to as the Settlement Act, established the principle that a specific parish was responsible for providing poor relief to each individual, known as their parish of settlement. Criteria for obtaining a settlement in a parish included paying rent of £10 or more per annum, serving an apprenticeship and being hired to work for a year and a day. Some long-term residents, such as agricultural day labourers and their families, might have lived in a parish for many years but not obtained a settlement there because they had not fulfilled any of the relevant criteria. If they applied for poor relief, referred to as becoming *chargeable*, their parish of settlement would be responsible for providing for them. In most cases, the individual or family would be returned to their parish of settlement, known as *removal*, but in some cases the parish of settlement would agree to pay the costs involved in their maintenance in the parish where they were living, particularly for short periods.

There is evidence that the Poor Law worked reasonably well in areas with little movement of population, and people in need were often treated relatively humanely. However, towards the end of the eighteenth century, as the population increased and people became more mobile, the system began to break down. In many instances the parish of settlement could not be established with certainty, or was open to dispute. Legitimate children automatically took the settlement of their father until such time as they obtained a settlement of their own. Adults who had not obtained their own settlement retained the settlement of their father, and sometimes even inherited the settlement of their grandfather. A woman took her husband's settlement on marriage and a widow retained her late husband's settlement. This was particularly significant if a woman married a man while he was serving away from his home area as a soldier, sailor or militiaman. If the couple subsequently settled in the wife's parish and the husband died without having obtaining a settlement there, the wife and any children were liable to be removed to the husband's parish of settlement. A widow who remarried took her new husband's settlement, but her children by the earlier marriage retained their late father's settlement. This could result in a mother and any children over the age of seven being removed to different parishes.

Poor relief was paid for by the more prosperous parish inhabitants who paid poor rates based on the value of the land they owned or occupied. The poor rate was set by the parish Vestry, which represented ratepayers and so tried to keep the rates as low as possible. Many parishes were therefore reluctant to allow poor people from elsewhere to come to live there, as they could subsequently apply for relief and become chargeable, and it might be difficult to establish their parish of settlement. This concern could be eliminated if the individual or family obtained a *settlement certificate* from their parish of settlement, confirming that the parish acknowledged responsibility for them as settled inhabitants. Settlement certificates were issued by the Overseers of the Poor of the parish acknowledging settlement and countersigned by two Justices of the Peace. Following an Act of 1795 people could no longer be removed from a parish unless they had actually become chargeable.

When an individual or family applied for poor relief in a parish in which they did not have a settlement, the Overseers applied to magistrates for a *removal order*, to enable them to be legally removed to their parish of settlement. If not already known this was established in a *settlement examination*. This involved the head of the family being asked questions under oath by two magistrates and the answers being recorded. The resulting document summarized relevant details of their life history, including place of birth, parishes in which they had lived and worked, and any criteria by which they might have previously obtained a settlement. If they had not obtained a settlement of their own, they would also be asked questions about the person whose settlement they had inherited, usually a father or husband. For individuals or families who had been constantly on the move, with many changes of employment, it was often difficult to establish the last parish in which they, or the person whose settlement they had inherited, had obtained a settlement. In the absence of other evidence, the adjudgement of an individual's place of settlement was based entirely on the information they provided under oath, some of which may have been incorrect as a result of either faulty memory or deliberate deception.

A removal order, signed by two magistrates, required the Churchwardens and Overseers of the parish of residence to convey the individual or family to their parish of settlement, and the Churchwardens and Overseers there to receive and provide for them. In many cases there was no doubt about the parish of settlement, but in other cases the Overseers of the destination parish disputed that their parish was the parish of settlement and issued a notice of appeal. Disputes between parishes that could not otherwise be resolved were adjudicated at Quarter Sessions.

Although the principles under which the Old Poor Law operated remained substantially the same, various changes were made during the course of the Georgian era. From the late seventeenth century some parishes, towns and cities set up workhouses by means of local acts. Bristol was the first city to establish a Corporation of the Poor in 1696. The Corporation operated a poor relief system for all the city parishes, and about thirty towns and cities set up similar systems during the eighteenth century. The Poor Law made a distinction between the impotent poor, including the aged and infirm and widows with small children, and the able-bodied poor who were capable of work. Knatchbull's General Workhouse Act of 1723 permitted parishes to set up workhouses and to apply the 'workhouse test', whereby relief could be withheld from those unwilling to enter a workhouse, but the majority of paupers continued to receive relief in their own homes. Gilbert's Act of 1782 was intended to be more humane, and provided for groups of parishes to form unions to set up poor houses, intended only for children, the old, the sick and the infirm. The able-bodied poor were to be provided with either relief in their own homes or employment. Relatively few unions were set up, and most poor relief in rural areas continued to be provided by individual parishes.

War with France and a series of poor harvests resulted in high bread prices in early 1795, which led to food riots. The Berkshire magistrates who met at the Pelican Inn in Speenhamland on 6 May 1795 acknowledged that 'the present state of the poor does require further assistance than has generally been given them'. Although magistrates were empowered to regulate wages, they chose to introduce a system of supplementary allowances, based on the price of bread and the size of men's families, to be paid for out of the poor rates. The 'Speenhamland System' was rapidly adopted elsewhere, particularly in the agricultural counties of the south of England. Although this system of allowances saved families from starvation, it resulted in many employers reducing wages even further, as they knew that the wages they paid would be supplemented from the poor rates. Not only did poor rates increase dramatically, but owners and occupiers who paid poor rates but did not employ labourers ended up subsidizing farmers who did, most of whom could have afforded to pay higher wages. Expenditure on poor relief almost trebled from £2.6 million in 1792 to £6.5 million in 1812. In 1800 about 28 per cent of the population in England was in receipt of poor relief.

The end of the Napoleonic Wars in 1815 was followed by a severe depression in both agriculture and manufacturing. Former soldiers and sailors re-entered the labour market, increasing unemployment. Although manufacturing recovered fairly rapidly, the agricultural depression was deep and lasting. The increasing expenditure on poor relief led to a review of the Poor Laws, culminating in two acts known as the Sturges Bourne Acts. The first act of 1818 gave multiple votes to some Vestry members on a sliding scale depending on the amount of property they owned or occupied. The second act of 1819 permitted parishes to set up Select Vestries, of between five and twenty principal inhabitants, with specific responsibility for poor relief. Members were to be chosen by the open Vestry on an annual basis. Select Vestries were set up in many parishes and almost three thousand had been established by 1828.

Overseers of the Poor also had responsibility for the apprenticeship of poor children and pursuing the fathers of bastards for maintenance payments (discussed later in this chapter).

Burlison (2009) describes the Poor Law from the perspective of family history researchers, and provides an overview of sources. Detailed descriptions of Poor Law records can be found in Tate (1969) and Hawkings (2011).

Records of Settlement and Removal

The Poor Law records most likely to contain genealogical information are the three separate documents relating to individuals and their families: *settlement certificates*, *settlement examinations* and *removal orders*. These were often produced in duplicate or triplicate and, if they have survived, can potentially be found in various different collections in local archives, for example parish, Petty Sessions and Quarter Sessions records. Of the three types of document, removal orders survive in the greatest numbers, with fewer settlement examinations and settlement certificates surviving.

Removal orders did not record place of birth, but confirm that an individual had previously obtained a settlement in the parish to which they were being removed. The names of all members of the family were usually recorded, including the names and ages of children. A typical removal order from 1736 contains the following relevant information:

- The Churchwardens and Overseers of Morland in Westmorland complained to the local magistrates that Thomas Gibbons, Elizabeth his wife and their three children William aged about 10 years, Mary aged about 8 years and George aged about 3 years were living in their parish, where they did not have a settlement, and had now become chargeable.
- The magistrates examined Thomas Gibbons and established that his last place of legal settlement was at High Braithwaite in the parish of St Mary's Without the Walls of Carlisle in Cumberland.
- The magistrates issued a removal order requiring the Churchwardens and Overseers of Morland to convey the family to High Braithwaite, and the Chapelwardens and Overseers there to receive and provide for them as inhabitants of their parish.

Settlement certificates usually named family members and indicated the parishes of settlement and residence. A typical certificate from 1766 contains the following information:

- To: the Churchwardens and Overseers of Claverdon in Warwickshire (the parish where the family were living or intended to live, but did not have a settlement).
- From: the Churchwardens and Overseers of Barby in Northamptonshire, confirming that they'own and acknowledge' Richard Sheasby and Mary his wife and John, Jane and William their children to be inhabitants legally settled in their parish.

Removal orders and settlement certificates provide information about an individual's last place of legal settlement. In some cases this was their parish of birth, enabling a baptism to be found and other family members to be identified. When it was not their parish of birth, it may not be obvious how the settlement had been obtained without an accompanying settlement examination. Settlement examinations are the most valuable surviving source of information on poorer members of society, as they usually record places of birth, as far as was known to the examinant (an archaic term for the person being examined), and places they had lived and worked. Details of the place and approximate date of marriage and names and ages of children were also often recorded. When the person being examined had not obtained a settlement in their own right, information about the person whose settlement they had taken would also be recorded. Settlement examinations therefore provide biographical information about people from a sector of society for which very little information was otherwise recorded, and a single settlement examination may contain a great deal of information, as in the following example:

> The Examination of Mary Clench now residing in the Town of Blandford Forum in the said County [of Dorset] widow taken on oath before us two of His Majesty's Justices of the Peace in and for the said county this [blank] day of [blank] 1782 touching the place of her legal settlement.
>
> This examinant on her oath saith that she was born at Romsey in the County of Hampshire about twenty nine years ago where her parents were then legally settled as she has heard and believed, that she resided with her father at Romsey aforesaid until she was about seventeen years old when she married with one Robert Bond who then resided in Romsey aforesaid, a baker. That soon after their marriage her said husband enlisted into the Marines, where he continued about six months when he was discharged, and leaving this examinant his wife at Romsey with her friends he went to Gosport in the said County of Hampshire where this examinant soon after heard that he died. That she continued with her friends at Romsey near eight years afterwards when she married one George Clench at Romsey aforesaid then a private in

the Hampshire Militia where he continued till about April last past when she the examinant went with her husband to London where they continued about three months and then her said husband left her and she returned to Romsey aforesaid where she continued till December last past when she was removed by an order of two Justices to Blandford aforesaid with one child by her said last husband aged about two years named Sophia, that she had a letter about five weeks ago from one Richard Clench of Bristol her cousin to inform her that her husband was dead, and that she never heard him say nor does she know his place of settlement and that she has not since done any act to gain a settlement to her knowledge.

As well as removal orders, settlement certificates and settlement examinations, other records relating to the operation of the Poor Law may have survived, such as accounts of expenditure of the Overseers, known as Overseers' accounts. These may include details of regular payments to the elderly and infirm, and to widows with young children, and irregular payments to other inhabitants following illness, accident or other misfortune. Records of payments for paupers' funerals may enable burial records containing only minimal information to be correlated with specific individuals. Overseers' accounts may also enable removals to be identified in the absence of surviving removal orders.

In some parishes the records of Poor Law expenditure were recorded in Churchwardens' accounts, which can be worth consulting when no specific Overseers' accounts are available. Constables' accounts have sometimes survived, and may record the expenses involved in conveying individuals and families to their parish of settlement. The information recorded in Vestry minutes is very variable and many contain minimal references to Poor Law business apart from the annual appointment of Overseers. However, the minutes of the Select Vestries established after 1819 routinely recorded decisions concerning the granting or refusal of poor relief and the amounts paid to individual paupers.

In many counties, routine Poor Law matters were handled by magistrates at Petty Sessions, but relatively few records have survived for the Georgian era, with none surviving for some counties. Disputes between parishes relating to settlement and removal were referred to Quarter Sessions for a final decision. Poor Law litigation was at its height in the period from 1815 to 1834, when a significant proportion of the business of Quarter Sessions throughout the country was related to Poor Law disputes. Decisions of the court were usually recorded in *order books*. It was also common practice for copies of loose documents presented to the court, such as removal orders, bastardy orders and settlement examinations, to be rolled up and stored as *Quarter Sessions rolls*. These have survived for many counties, as well as those cities and boroughs that held their own Quarter Sessions. Poor Law documents may be found in Quarter Sessions records when the corresponding copies have not survived in parish records.

Parish Apprenticeship Records

Poor Law *apprenticeship indentures* have sometimes survived in parish records. Parish or pauper apprenticeships were quite different to normal apprenticeships, sometimes referred to as voluntary apprenticeships (discussed in Chapter 6). Pauper apprenticeships were arranged so that poor children, or their families, did not become a financial burden on parishes. Unlike voluntary apprenticeships, most of which related to boys, pauper apprenticeships were arranged for both boys and girls. One or both parents may have died, the parents may have been very poor with a large number of children to support, or the child may have been a bastard. Children could be apprenticed from the age of 7, until the age of 24 before 1766, and 21 thereafter. Although some boys were apprenticed to tradesmen such as weavers, coopers, blacksmiths or shoemakers, it was common for boys in rural parishes to be apprenticed to learn 'the art and science of husbandry' and girls to learn 'the art and mystery of a housewife', which in reality meant working either as an agricultural labourer or a domestic servant.

Overseers were keen to arrange apprenticeships in different parishes so that poor children would subsequently gain settlements elsewhere and not in their own parish. Unlike conventional apprenticeship indentures, those for pauper children rarely included the names of parents. The information recorded usually included only the name of the apprentice and sometimes his or her age, the name of the master and his abode, together with the names of the parish officers and the magistrates authorizing the apprenticeship. A small proportion of apprentices came to be treated like adopted children, but others were treated harshly and used as a source of cheap labour. As well as being apprenticed to individuals, pauper children were increasingly used as a source of cheap labour in mills during the Industrial Revolution. A third of the workers in some cotton mills were pauper apprentices, many brought in from outside the local area. Overseers in London parishes sent children to work in mills outside the capital, particularly in the Midlands and the north, and even when one or both parents were still alive they were not always told where their children had been sent.

Although Poor Law apprenticeship indentures contain little genealogical information, they may enable links between parishes of birth and settlement to be established. They may also provide an indication of a family's social status. Records of the binding of apprentices may also be found in Vestry minutes and Overseers' accounts. Parishes were required to keep registers of apprentices from 1802. These registers have survived for many parishes, and usually contain more information than the corresponding indentures, including the names of parents. Some disputes regarding apprenticeships were referred to Quarter Sessions.

Bastardy Records

Children born outside of marriage can be identified from baptism records, in which they were usually referred to as bastards, illegitimate or base born. Bastards usually took the surname of their mother, with the majority of baptism records including only her name, often qualified with a description such as single woman or spinster, and without the name of the father being recorded. Some clergyman recorded the father's name when it was known.

Before 1834 the place of settlement of bastard children was their parish of birth. Overseers tried to prevent the mothers of bastards from becoming chargeable to their parish whenever possible. When they discovered that an unmarried woman was pregnant, they would often try to persuade the father to marry her. Intervals between marriage and baptism of a first child indicate that a significant proportion of women must have been visibly pregnant when they married, but it is impossible to know how many of these couples planned to marry in any event. When parents remained unmarried, Overseers pursued fathers for the financial support of mothers and children. The identities of the fathers of bastards can therefore sometimes be established from Poor Law records even when not recorded in baptism records. However, the survival of bastardy records is very variable, and informal financial arrangements may have been made in many cases, without any official documents having been drawn up.

There were several different types of bastardy record. A father acknowledging paternity often entered into a *bastardy bond*, legally binding him to support the mother and child. Women were examined by magistrates in *bastardy examinations* to establish fathers' identities. Men identified as being the fathers of bastards were ordered to appear before magistrates and issued with maintenance orders, and were summonsed to appear at Quarter Sessions if they failed to comply. Bastardy examinations are usually the most informative documents, as they often record the date and place of birth of the child and provide details of the place of abode and occupation of the putative father, as well as sometimes including a settlement examination for the mother. Documents relating to bastardy may be found in parish records, Petty Sessions records and Quarter Sessions records.

Further information on records relating to bastardy can be found in Tate (1969) and Paley (2004).

Searching for Poor Law Records

Poor Law material may be distributed between several different record collections in archives: parish records, Petty Sessions records and Quarter Sessions records. Most surviving parish records have now been deposited in local archives, but the survival of Poor Law material is often a matter of chance. There are no surviving Poor Law records for some parishes, but they have survived in great quantity for others. As was mentioned in Chapter 2, the historical civil and ecclesiastical records of parishes came under separate ownership in 1894, so the two categories of record for some parishes may now be held in different archives, particularly in urban areas. However, any records containing both types of material, such as many Vestry minutes and composite volumes of Churchwardens' and Overseers' accounts, remained church property, so they are held with the ecclesiastical records. In those areas where civil and ecclesiastical parish records are held in different archives, there is therefore a possibility that material relevant to the Poor Law may be held in both. Archive websites can often be helpful in establishing the location of Poor Law material for specific parishes, but it may sometimes be necessary to contact archives directly to establish exactly what material they hold. It is also advisable to investigate the records of neighbouring counties when poor individuals or their families lived close to county boundaries.

The extent to which parish Poor Law material has been listed varies between archives. Individual documents, such as settlement examinations, settlement certificates, removal orders and apprenticeship indentures, have been listed individually in some archives' online catalogues and the Discovery catalogue. Some collections of Poor Law records, such as those for Dorset, have been digitized by online search services. The only search tools for Poor Law records in some archives are typescript listings or card indexes only available at the archive premises. Some indexes have been produced by local family history societies, and these are usually available for purchase, and may also be available for consultation in libraries and archives. Identifying individual items when no search tools currently exist requires establishing whether records have survived for relevant parishes and browsing through the individual documents. However, the identification of relevant material in the records of unexpected parishes may only be possible when new search tools become available or after further clues have been found.

Some sources such as Overseers' accounts and Vestry minutes have been transcribed, but otherwise searching for information relating to individuals and families in sources of this type requires browsing page by page through original handwritten records. The registers of apprenticeship indentures introduced in 1802 have been transcribed and indexed by family history societies in some areas.

Some search tools for identifying names in surviving Petty Sessions records may be available. The extent to which names recorded in Quarter Sessions records can be searched varies from one archive to another. The Quarter Sessions records held by some archives have been indexed by name, and these can be searched using archives' online catalogues or card indexes available at archive premises. The Quarter Sessions records held in other archives have either not been name indexed at all, or only for specific periods. Quarter Sessions records are of potential interest to historians as well as genealogists, and large collections that were previously unindexed sometimes become searchable as a result of externally funded cataloguing projects. Name indexes to Poor Law material in Quarter Sessions records have also been produced by some individuals and family history societies. In the absence of search tools, finding records relating to specific individuals in such large collections is only feasible if the dates of events can be established from other sources.

Chapter 10

LAND AND PROPERTY

Records concerning ownership and occupation of land sometimes contain a significant amount of information about individuals and families. Deeds and manorial records may contain information about the land owned or occupied by families, and often include details of relationships between family members. Deeds were usually written on large sheets of parchment, which were then folded up. Records of this type have rarely been microfilmed or digitized, and the extent to which individual items have been listed in archive catalogues is also very variable. Copies or digital images of items that have been identified from archive catalogues can often be ordered, but otherwise using records of this type requires either visiting the archives where they are held, or employing a specialist researcher.

The enclosure of land was at its height during the Georgian era, and enclosure records can provide a great deal of information about the land people owned, although they rarely contain genealogical information.

RECORDS OF LAND OWNERSHIP AND OCCUPATION

Owners and occupiers of land paid taxes, rates and tithes, and some were eligible to serve on juries. The related records (discussed in other chapters) can provide an indication of where more prosperous ancestors lived, and changes in the names recorded over a period of time can sometimes provide clues to genealogical relationships. Deeds and manorial records, when they survive, usually go a stage further, describing land holdings in some detail and often referring to relationships between family members. Such records can be particularly valuable when researching families who were sufficiently prosperous to own land, but for whom the amount of information that can be gleaned from wills and administrations is minimal.

Most land in England is now registered with the Land Registry, and once land has been registered there is no further requirement for deeds to be kept. Deeds that are no longer required have either been disposed of or preserved as historic documents, and solicitors are now encouraged to deposit redundant deeds in local archives. As well as in collections of deeds deposited by solicitors, deeds can also be found in the records of landowning families. Many of these records have now been deposited in local archives, but some are still in the possession of the families concerned. Archivists are employed in some private archives, such as those at Alnwick Castle and Longleat House, and some offer a paid research service. Many historical land records are also held in college archives of the universities of Oxford and Cambridge and in cathedral archives.

Title deeds are legal agreements concerning *real property*, which consists of land and any associated buildings, crops and other immovable features resulting from human activity. There were three main types of property tenure during the Georgian era: freehold, leasehold and copyhold. *Freehold* was essentially ownership of property for ever, *leasehold* was the grant of a property to a tenant for a specified period of time, and *copyhold* related to property that was part of a manor, which like freehold property could be bought, sold or inherited. Freehold and leasehold still exist today, but copyhold was gradually replaced by freehold tenure and finally abolished in 1925.

Many deeds are agreements between unrelated individuals and contain no genealogical information, but some include the names of two or more members of the same family and a small proportion contain a considerable amount of genealogical detail. Genealogical information may be found in the names of the parties to the deed, the names of individuals referred to in the summary or 'recital' of previous transactions and events relating to the property, and the names of previous owners or occupiers referred to in the description of the property.

Freehold property held in *fee simple* could be sold, but property in *fee tail* could only be inherited by an heir. Such a legal restriction was referred to as an *entail* and the current owner of the property as a *tenant for life* (the effect of entails on inheritance is discussed in Chapter 8). The ownership of freehold property could be transferred through a variety of legal procedures, such as *feoffment, quitclaim, bargain and sale* and *lease and release*. The most common method in the Georgian era was the lease and release. The documents produced consisted of a lease for a year for a nominal amount and a much larger and more detailed document known as a release, dated the following day. The lease was often stored inside the release, but sometimes only one of the two documents has survived.

When a property was sold, an *abstract of title* was often produced, which summarized the deeds relating to the property in chronological order. Abstracts of title are more succinct than the deeds themselves and generally include the genealogical information from several deeds in a single document. Abstracts of title may include information from deeds that are missing, and are sometimes found without any accompanying deeds.

In contrast to some other countries, no national system for recording land ownership existed in England until compulsory registration by the Land Registry was gradually implemented during the twentieth century. However, in the early eighteenth

Part of a deed from 1764. Many deeds and other legal documents were written in distinctive scripts, but the styles used were fairly uniform. It is possible to learn to read them with practice, and many professional genealogists provide transcription services.

century, registries for the voluntary registration of deeds were established in the West, East and North Ridings of Yorkshire and in Middlesex. Some deeds were also registered or *enrolled* in the courts of law.

Leasehold tenure was the grant of a property to a tenant for a specified period of time in exchange for payment. The specified period of time could be either a fixed number of years or the lifetimes of named individuals. The latter type of lease, known as a *lease for lives*, expired when all the named individuals had died. Leases for three lives were particularly common in the south-west of England, where they were combined with a term of years, usually ninety-nine. The named individuals were often the tenant and two much younger family members, whose ages were sometimes recorded. It was common practice to renew the lease when one person died, replacing them by a younger family member, and the repetition of this process could enable a property to be held by the same family in perpetuity. A series of leases for three lives for the same property can often contain information on several generations of a family. Even if the leases themselves have not survived, the records of larger estates may include lease books in which they were summarized. The information recorded in leases for lives can be particularly valuable when researching people for whom probate records are less likely to be found, such as small tenant farmers.

Copyhold tenure related to property that was part of a manor, and like freehold property it could be bought, sold or inherited. Copyhold land was conveyed by the tenant surrendering his land to the Lord of the Manor at the Court Baron, followed by the admission of the new tenant. These transactions were recorded in the *court roll*, and a copy of the relevant entry was given to the new tenant as the equivalent of a title deed. Land held in this way was therefore known as copyhold, and the copies can often be found in bundles of deeds. Manor courts were presided over by stewards, who were usually lawyers, so the records of manor courts are often very similar.

The survival of deeds and manorial records is quite random and they are not always well catalogued. Deeds and manorial records are not necessarily held in the areas where the land was situated, but may be held in archives where the records of the family or organization that originally owned the land have been deposited. Deeds that have been separately listed can usually be identified by searching for relevant names using the Discovery catalogue and individual archive catalogues, but many collections of deeds have not been listed. Finding relevant deeds may therefore require identifying unlisted collections relating to parishes or villages where ancestors are known to have lived and browsing through them. Such speculative searching has the potential to enable many relevant records to be discovered but can be time-consuming and is often fruitless.

The location of manorial records can be established using the Manorial Documents Register (MDR), maintained by TNA. Records for the majority of counties are included in the Discovery catalogue, and a dedicated MDR home page enables searching by manor name and parish name. Establishing the location of manorial records for counties not yet searchable online requires either using indexes on microfilm at TNA or submitting an enquiry.

The various types of deed are described in a small pamphlet by Wormleighton (2012), and in a more detailed book by Alcock (2017). There is also a comprehensive guide to deeds on the website of Manuscripts and Special Collections at the University of Nottingham. Most books on manorial records have been written for local historians and give more prominence to the records of the Middle Ages. The most accessible introduction to manorial records for family history researchers is a pamphlet by Forrest (2011), which despite its title is actually a general introduction to manorial records in which records from Dorset have been used as examples.

Fire insurance companies based in London, such as the Sun and Royal Exchange, insured properties throughout the country during the Georgian era. Although the records contain no genealogical information, they can provide information about people's occupations, addresses, and the types of dwelling they lived and worked in. Many of these records are held at London Metropolitan Archives (LMA) and some have been indexed by name and can be searched on Discovery and LMA's online catalogue. Further information on fire

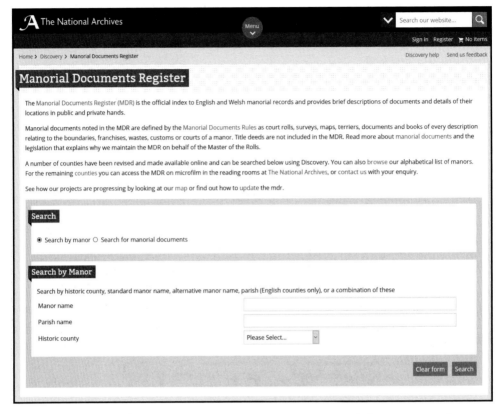

The Manorial Documents Register *home page. Manorial documents can be identified by manor name and by parish.*

insurance records as a source of family history information can be found in Hawkings (2003).

ENCLOSURE RECORDS

Land was traditionally farmed under the open field system, in which each landowner held strips of land in several fields. Enclosure involved redistributing land so that each landowner held a discrete area of land, which was subsequently enclosed by a hedge, fence or wall. As well as open fields, common lands and wastes were included in this redistribution. Enclosure affected people at all levels of society, and its effect on migration is discussed in Chapter 12. Before the mid-eighteenth century, enclosure often took place by informal agreement or by enrolling agreements in the courts of law. The process of parliamentary enclosure, which was at its height between 1760 and 1830, involved the appointment of commissioners, who surveyed the parish to be enclosed, heard claims and allotted land. Their final decision was summarized in a legally binding document known as an *enclosure award*.

Enclosure awards, and accompanying maps, record the ownership of land and include details of the land they held both before and after enclosure. Copies of enclosure awards may be found in parish records and Quarter Sessions records, held in local archives, but their survival varies by county. Enclosure records for some counties, such as Berkshire, Norfolk and Worcestershire, have been digitized and are freely available online. When used in conjunction with other sources, such as leases and Land Tax records, enclosure awards can indicate the land that people occupied as well as the land that people owned. Further information on enclosure records can be found in Hollowell (2000).

Further discussion of maps is beyond the scope of this book. Information about the range of maps produced during the Georgian era, including estate, manorial, enclosure and tithe maps, and published maps, can be found in Masters (2009) and Hindle (1998). Tithe records are described in Kain and Prince (2000).

Chapter 11

LAW AND ORDER

People living today are likely to have at least one ancestor who fell foul of the law during the Georgian era, and some may have several. The criminal justice system in Georgian England and the sources for researching ancestors who became caught up in it are outlined in this chapter. The records of civil disputes in the equity courts, often referred to as Chancery Proceedings, are also discussed. Many civil disputes were between people who were related, so Chancery Proceedings can be a rich source of genealogical information, particularly for middle-class families.

CRIME

Before police forces began to be established at the very end of the Georgian era, crime was kept under control by Parish Constables and Justices of the Peace. Special Constables were sometimes sworn in by magistrates, usually in response to civil disturbances, and the military was called in to control more serious disorder. Sentences were harsh, with many relatively minor offences punishable by imprisonment, transportation or death. Although some crimes were committed by hardened criminals and planned in advance, it is likely that many thefts were opportunistic, committed out of desperation when times were hard. People were tried not only for crimes that are still committed today, such as murder, manslaughter, assault, theft, rape and forgery, but also for a range of other offences such as poaching, rioting and sedition (discussed below). Several books are available describing the wide range of sources available for researching criminal ancestors, although none focus specifically on the Georgian era. Wade (2009) is organized according to the type of offence, and Hawkings (2009) and Oates (2017) describe the sources. Court records are described in Raymond (2016).

Many people appeared before the courts for poaching during the Georgian era. Although some poaching was carried out by gangs of professional criminals, most poachers were otherwise law-abiding lower-class men who did not consider killing wild animals for food to be wrong when food was scarce and prices were high. The sporting rights of the upper class were protected by game laws, which became increasingly punitive as time went on. The game laws were enforced by Justices of the Peace, who were themselves from the landowning class that benefited from them. A man convicted of poaching could be sentenced to several months' imprisonment, but more severe sentences, including transportation, were gradually introduced after 1815. Sentences were particularly severe when poachers operated in armed gangs, and men who caused injury to gamekeepers were liable to the death penalty. Around a quarter of the prison population in the early nineteenth century were offenders against the game laws.

A significant number of people were tried for insurrection and taking part in riots. Most riots were spontaneous, fuelled by a collective feeling of injustice relating to changes over which people felt they had no control, as few people were able to vote. Over 400 riots took place during the eighteenth century, with grain and bread riots accounting for over half of recorded disturbances after 1750. Riots took place in response to the introduction of turnpikes, the militia ballot, the enclosure of land, and the introduction of machinery that put people out of work and reduced wages.

The new militia system introduced in 1757, based on balloting, was perceived as a form of conscription by lower-class men and their families, as they could not afford to buy themselves out, and militia riots took place in many parts of the country during the following years. The introduction of the new system had met fierce resistance elsewhere in Northumberland and Durham, so there was a large military presence for the balloting of men at Hexham in March 1761, where a demonstration resulted in about fifty people being killed and three hundred injured. The soldiers who fired on the demonstrators were themselves members of the North Yorkshire Militia.

The anti-Catholic Gordon riots in London in 1780 resulted in the destruction of many buildings and the greatest number of casualties of any eighteenth-century riot.

The Luddite disturbances against the introduction of machinery in 1811 and 1812, when Wellington's army was fighting in the Peninsula, involved over ten thousand soldiers being stationed in the textile areas of the Midlands and north of England. Machine breaking became a capital offence in 1812, for which seventeen men were hanged the following year. Low wages for agricultural labourers in the arable areas of the south of England, unemployment and the introduction of agricultural machines, led to the Swing riots of 1830, after which hundreds of men were imprisoned and transported and nineteen were hanged.

People were also tried for engaging in activities that would now be regarded as rights, such as expressing controversial opinions and associating with others to try to improve wages and working conditions or to campaign for the reform of Parliament.

The Gordon Riots in London in 1780. Riots were relatively frequent during the Georgian era.

The government of William Pitt feared revolution in England after the French Revolution of 1789. During the 1790s members of radical but peaceful organizations, such as the London Corresponding Society, were charged with treason and sedition, but demands for parliamentary reform continued to grow. Several people were killed and many more wounded in 1819 when cavalry charged a peaceful crowd demonstrating for reform at St Peter's Fields in Manchester. This event, four years after the Battle of Waterloo, became known as the Peterloo Massacre. In 1831, the year before the Great Reform Act came into force, the reluctance of Parliament to reform the system of parliamentary representation resulted in riots in several towns, including Nottingham and Bristol.

Collective action by workers to improve their wages and conditions was suppressed through legislation. In 1834 agricultural labourers from Tolpuddle in Dorset who had formed themselves into a friendly society were transported for taking an illegal oath of secrecy. This was followed by widespread protests and a petition to Parliament. The men, who became known as the Tolpuddle Martyrs, were eventually pardoned and returned to England.

As well as court records (discussed below), many different sources are held at TNA relating to people who took part in civil disturbances or were known or believed to hold radical views that the government considered to be dangerous. Some records relating to individuals can be identified using the Discovery catalogue.

THE CRIMINAL COURTS

Individual Justices of the Peace were empowered to deal with minor offences. Their actions were not officially recorded, but they were encouraged to keep their own records, some of which have survived and been deposited in archives. Records of this type are of historical interest, so some have been transcribed and published.

As mentioned in Chapter 2, Courts Leet persisted into the Georgian era in some manorial boroughs. They dealt with minor offences such as obstructing water courses and depositing piles of dung in the street. Surviving records are usually held in local archives, and can be a rich source of information about individuals at all levels of society. Records of this type are of interest to local historians, so many have been transcribed and indexed, and some transcriptions can be found online.

By the late eighteenth century it was common practice for counties to be divided into specific areas that later became known as Petty Sessional Divisions, with Petty Sessions held in a town in each area on a regular basis to deal with minor crimes, such as drunkenness and breaches of the peace, and also with Poor Law matters. Petty Sessions were presided over by two magistrates, and later developed into magistrates' courts. Relatively few Petty Sessions records have survived from the Georgian era, but there is considerable variation between counties. Surviving records are held in local archives, and information on holdings can usually be found on archive websites. Petty Sessions records relating to crimes have rarely been indexed by name, so finding records for individuals is usually dependent on discovering clues in other sources.

More serious crimes were tried at Quarter Sessions and Assizes. Although there was some overlap, the most serious offences, including capital offences, were tried at Assizes. At the end of the eighteenth century over two hundred offences were punishable by death. A death sentence was mandatory for certain offences, but became discretionary for all crimes except murder and treason after 1823.

Quarter Sessions were presided over by the Justices of the Peace of the relevant county or borough, and were held at Epiphany (January), Easter (March/April), Midsummer (July) and Michaelmas (September). County Quarter Sessions were held either in the county town or rotated around the major towns in the county. Separate Quarter Sessions were also held in many cities and boroughs, and were sometimes referred to as Borough Sessions. Some of these towns were also locations for the county Quarter Sessions. Two sets of Quarter Sessions could therefore potentially be sitting in the same town at virtually the same time. For example, Quarter Sessions for the County of Devon, held at the Castle in Exeter, usually overlapped with those for the City of Exeter, held at the Guildhall. Researchers who have found a newspaper report for an individual who appeared at Quarter Sessions in a specific town on a certain date, and are unaware of the existence of the two different courts, may fail to find further relevant information in archives because they were looking in the wrong set of records.

Assizes were held in most counties twice a year, during Lent and Summer. They were presided over by professional judges from London, who travelled round the country, which was divided into six circuits. The Old Bailey was the criminal court for London and Middlesex. It became the Central Criminal Court, with wider jurisdiction, in 1834. The palatinates of Cheshire, Lancashire and Durham held their own Assizes.

Many trials and convictions at Quarter Sessions and Assizes, together with some at Petty Sessions towards the end of the Georgian era, were reported in local newspapers, a large number of which have now been digitized. However, the searchable text has been produced by Optical Character Recognition (OCR), and is often inaccurate, so some of the names mentioned may not be findable. Name indexes to some local newspapers are available in local studies libraries and archives.

The amount of detail recorded in newspaper reports of trials generally increased as the Georgian era progressed, and fairly lengthy reports of minor but unusual crimes can sometimes be found in early nineteenth century newspapers. Proceedings of the Old Bailey were published shortly after each sitting, and these records have now been digitized and can be searched on the *Proceedings of the Old Bailey, 1674-1913* website.

People who were tried at Quarter Sessions and Assizes after 1805 (1791 in Middlesex) can be identified using centralized Home Office *Criminal Registers*, now held at TNA in series HO 26 and HO 27. These records, which can be searched on both Ancestry and Findmypast, include the name of the accused, their age, a brief description of the crime (e.g. larceny), the date and place of the trial, and whether they were sentenced (to death, transportation or imprisonment) or acquitted. Sources such as Criminal Registers and newspaper reports include the dates and locations of trials. Once the date and place of a trial have been established, it is usually possible to find further information in relevant court records held in archives.

Quarter Sessions records are held in archives in the areas concerned. The types of records produced by each court of Quarter Sessions varied. Individual documents presented to the court provide the greatest amount of detail about crimes, and these were usually rolled up at the end of each sitting and stored as *Quarter Sessions rolls*. Detailed statements made by the accused and witnesses, known as *depositions*, are often included. *Order books* summarize the details of crimes, verdicts, and sentences if found guilty. Not all the records that were made at the time have survived. No Quarter Sessions rolls survive for Cornwall, for example, although the contents of the order books have been transcribed and can be searched online. Large collections of Quarter Sessions rolls exist for many counties, but there is considerable variation in the extent to which the individual documents they contain have been name indexed. The main categories of record available for each court of Quarter Sessions in England are listed by county in Gibson (2007). Further information on the records available for specific Quarter Sessions can usually be found on archive websites.

Most Assize court records are now held at TNA. Records were kept at the time that were similar to those for Quarter Sessions, but they have been heavily weeded, so more detailed records such as depositions may no longer survive. Assize records have not been indexed by name, and most of those before 1733 are in Latin. Some records relating to Assizes, such as lists of prisoners for trial, were kept locally and are now held with Quarter Sessions records in local archives.

Many court records include a considerable amount of detail about crimes and where they were committed, and often record the ages of the accused, but they rarely include details of place of birth or any other genealogical information. It may only be possible to infer relationships between individuals from court records when two or more members of the same family were involved in the same crime. Establishing whether an individual who committed a crime was actually the same person as an ancestor with the same name is therefore not always straightforward.

Verdicts at Quarter Sessions and Assizes were established by juries. All jurors were men holding freehold or copyhold land over a certain value. Lists of men in each parish who were eligible to serve on juries were sent to the Clerk of the Peace. Surviving *jurors lists* (sometimes referred to as *freeholders lists*) are held in Quarter Sessions records. Individual returns from parishes were copied into books, and both sets of records may have survived. These lists can enable more prosperous parish inhabitants to be identified during periods for which no similar lists, such as lists of parish ratepayers or Land Tax records, are available. Some lists have been published and others are available online, such as those for Devon, available on the Friends of Devon Archives website.

PUNISHMENT

Long prison sentences for convicted criminals were unusual during the Georgian era, as people convicted of more serious crimes were either transported or executed. Executions were carried out in public, so the associated crimes were often reported in newspapers and in published accounts of historical events written by people who were alive at the time. Transportation could be for life, or for a period of years, usually seven or fourteen. Until the outbreak of the American War of Independence in 1775, most transportation was to the British colonies in North America. Over 50,000 people from the British Isles were transported, and two lists have been published (Coldham, 1988b and 2002). These have been digitized and can be searched on Ancestry.

Following the loss of the American colonies, old decommissioned warships known as *prison hulks*, mainly moored on the River Thames, were used for housing prisoners. It was subsequently decided that Australia should be used as a penal colony, and the 'First Fleet' of convicts sailed in 1787, arriving in Australia in 1788. When transportation came to an end in 1868, 165,000 convicts had been sent to Australia, mainly to New South Wales and Van Diemen's Land (Tasmania). Records relating to convict transportation are held in both England and Australia, and many have now been digitized. Further information on transportation records can be found in Hawkings (2012).

Although introduced as a temporary measure, prison hulks continued to be used to house prisoners until well into the Victorian era, often while they were awaiting transportation. Some convicts were sent to hulks in Bermuda after 1823, where they were employed in the naval dockyard. Records of prisoners on hulks were kept by the Home Office and many have now been digitized or transcribed.

Prisons, usually referred to as gaols, were used to house prisoners awaiting trial, awaiting transportation after conviction or serving short periods of imprisonment. Although the records are relatively brief, gaol records often provide information about prisoners that is not available in other records, sometimes including birthplace, a physical description and where they were subsequently sent. Each county had a county gaol, and cities and boroughs with their own Quarter Sessions also had gaols. Surviving gaol registers are usually held in archives where related Quarter Sessions records are held, and some have been indexed, transcribed or digitized. Information from gaol registers held in local archives that are not available online may enable some brick walls to be overcome.

Various other prison records are held at TNA and are included in a large collection on Findmypast entitled *England & Wales, Crime, Prisons & Punishment, 1770-1935*. This collection includes, for example, a calendar of over 800 prisoners held at the county gaol in Winchester in 1830 following the Swing riots, mentioned earlier in this chapter.

IMPRISONMENT FOR DEBT

People could be imprisoned for debt until well into the Victorian era, so a large proportion of prisoners were debtors, often tradesmen or professional people who had fallen on hard times. Prisons gradually became overcrowded with debtors, and Parliament passed insolvency Acts at regular intervals to discharge them on certain conditions. Debtors wishing to take the benefit of these Acts were listed in the *London Gazette*, which has been digitized and can be searched online. Some London prisons were specifically for debtors, including the Fleet, Marshalsea and King's Bench prisons. Debtors with some money could pay for privileges, and some conducted business and received visitors, or even lived a short distance outside the prison itself. Marriages at the Fleet Prison are discussed in Chapter 3. Charles Dickens based his novel *Little Dorrit* on the experiences of his father, imprisoned for debt in the Marshalsea Prison in 1824. TNA holds some records related to imprisoned debtors, and many of these records have now been digitized.

THE EQUITY COURTS

The equity courts dealt with civil disputes and were concerned with achieving an outcome that was morally right or 'equitable'. The main equity court was the Court of Chancery, so the records are often referred to as Chancery Proceedings. A person with a grievance (the plaintiff) had a *bill of complaint* drawn up by a lawyer, in which the nature of the grievance was explained, often in some detail. The defendant's lawyer then responded with an *answer* in which a response was given to each of the points raised by the plaintiff, either agreeing with what had been said or providing an alternative version of events. The plaintiff could respond with a *replication*, to which the defendant could respond with a *rejoinder*, and so on, until the specific issues of dispute had been established.

A significant proportion of middle- and upper-class families were involved in disputes in the equity courts during the Georgian era. Disputes between people who were related were usually over land, trusts, settlements or wills. Bills and answers may include summaries of genealogically rich records such as wills, and often include further genealogical information. It is often possible to construct a family tree of several generations from the documents relating to a single dispute. For example, a bill and answer relating to a dispute between two cousins over land owned by their grandfather might name all the individuals in each generation and include the dates of many relevant events. Chancery Proceedings are particularly relevant to research in Devon and Somerset, where the sources available for

The Court of Chancery. Many disputes relating to middle-class families can be found in its records, which are held at TNA.

researching middle-class families are more limited, as a result of the destruction of locally-proved wills in 1942.

Depositions were also taken from witnesses, who could be from all social classes. Deposition records include their ages, occupations, places of abode and how long they had lived there. These records can often provide considerable additional detail about the parties involved in disputes, but the names of witnesses cannot currently be searched, so information relating to ancestors who acted as witnesses is not easy to find.

All equity court records are held at TNA. They consist of large sheets of parchment which have usually been rolled up. Identifying records of cases involving specific individuals or families requires using a range of printed, manuscript and online search tools. Catalogue records for Chancery Proceedings are gradually being added to the

Discovery catalogue, and records for a significant proportion of cases can now be searched online. However, comprehensive searching of equity court records requires either spending time at TNA or employing a specialist researcher. Further information on the records of the equity courts can be found in Moore (2017).

Chapter 12

MIGRATION

One of the major challenges of genealogical research in the Georgian era is establishing a person's place of birth in the absence of census information. Understanding historical migration patterns, and considering the reasons why an individual or family might have relocated, can sometimes enable their most likely areas of origin to be identified. It may then be possible to find evidence in the records of one of those areas, such as the will of a relative who had remained there. Migration patterns can also provide clues to the possible destinations of individuals or families who suddenly seem to 'disappear'.

Migration could involve relocation to another parish three miles away, a town 30 miles away, a different area 300 miles away, or another country, usually on a different continent. This chapter provides an outline of the main patterns of migration during the Georgian era, both within the British Isles and overseas.

MIGRATION WITHIN THE BRITISH ISLES

The population of England grew relatively slowly in the decades before 1750, but more than doubled between 1750 and 1837. The mobility of the population also increased dramatically during the same period, as a result of changes in agriculture, including the enclosure of land, the Industrial Revolution and long periods of war.

A series of inventions in the eighteenth century initiated the transformation of England from an agricultural into an industrial society. The use of coke instead of charcoal enabled iron and steel to be produced more cheaply and in larger quantities than previously, which led to the expansion of industries using iron as a raw material. At the beginning of the Georgian era, mills and factories relied on water power. The development of steam power enabled factories to be built in areas away from rivers, particularly where coal was readily available, many of which had previously been sparsely populated. Steam engines could also be used to pump out water from underground workings, enabling much deeper coal and metalliferous mines to be sunk.

At the beginning of the Georgian age most textile production took place in a domestic environment. Agricultural labouring work was seasonal, so many workers in rural areas also engaged in work that required some skill but could be learned fairly easily, such as spinning and weaving. Work was often carried out in family groups at home. From the mid-eighteenth century the textile industry was transformed by the invention of machines for spinning and weaving, although cottage industries and factories continued to coexist for several decades. Weavers and spinners had been relatively well paid

The iron bridge near Coalbrookdale in Shropshire, opened in 1781, the first major bridge in the world to be constructed from cast iron. New methods of iron production, together with many other developments in technology, resulted in migration to new industrial areas.

compared to agricultural labourers, but wages declined following the introduction of machinery.

Many agricultural labourers and small tenant farmers left rural areas as a result of changes in agriculture, and particularly after land had been enclosed. Most of the agricultural land that had not already been enclosed was enclosed between 1760 and 1830. The purpose of enclosure was to turn open fields, common lands and wastelands into more productive agricultural land. Enclosure Acts were usually initiated by large landowners, and there was often opposition from the smaller landowners and parish inhabitants without land of their own. The advantages and disadvantages of enclosure were debated at the time and have been argued over ever since. The main argument in favour of enclosure was that agricultural land became more efficient and productive, and the main argument against was that poor people without access to land became poorer.

During the first few decades of the Georgian period many farmers employed live-in farm servants on annual contracts. After they had saved enough money, these servants could marry and rent a cottage with the rights to use common land, and gradually rent strips of land of their own. Larger landowners bought up land during the Georgian era, so the size of farms gradually increased. Both the enclosure of land and the increase in the size of farms widened the gulf between farmers and labourers. Access to common land was reduced and labourers were hired for increasingly shorter periods. Many families who remained in rural areas and would previously have been able to support themselves subsisted on low wages and parish relief, particularly after 1815.

At the beginning of the Georgian era about 15 per cent of the English population lived in towns, and about half of urban dwellers lived in London, where the separate cities of London and Westminster became part of a larger conurbation into which villages on the outskirts were absorbed. The estimated population of London at the beginning of the Georgian era was 600,000, but other towns and cities were considerably smaller. Only five had populations of more than 10,000: Norwich (29,000), Bristol (20,000), Newcastle upon Tyne (18,000), Exeter (14,000) and York (12,000). Most towns

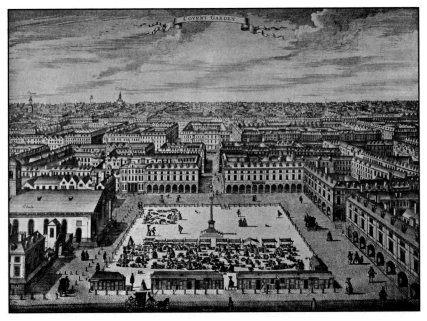

Covent Garden in 1720. In the early eighteenth century London was more than twenty times larger than Norwich, the next largest English city.

and cities had been established during the Middle Ages and were still relatively compact. Some still had walls within which most of their populations lived.

Steady migration from rural to urban areas occurred during the early Georgian period, but with the exception of people who moved to London, most people travelled relatively short distances, often to the nearest large town. Migration over longer distances increased after 1760 as a result of the Industrial Revolution. The majority of migrants were young adults and their destinations were determined by employment opportunities. Young women were drawn to work in towns and cities as domestic servants. The only English town that did not have a majority of women in 1801 was Oxford. By 1801 the population of London had grown to over a million. The ten largest towns in England in 1801 in order of size were: Liverpool, Manchester, Birmingham, Bristol, Leeds, Sheffield, Plymouth, Norwich, Bath and Portsmouth, but none had populations of more than 100,000.

Birmingham in 1783. Its population at that time was about 50,000.

Historians are now generally agreed that the major reasons for the growth in population after 1750 were earlier marriage resulting in larger families, and an increase in the proportion of people who married, as greater mobility provided more opportunities for meeting potential marriage partners.

A large proportion of the people living in London had not been born there. Evidence of their place of birth can sometimes be found in sources discussed in other chapters, such as apprenticeship and freedom records, wills, and Poor Law records. If further information cannot be found in local sources, the will of a family member who had moved to London could potentially contain information relating to the ancestry of an individual who had remained in the area concerned.

A further source recording the place of origin of some people living in London is the records of the British Lying-In Hospital in Holborn. This was a charity established in 1749 to provide maternity facilities for the lower class. Detailed records of admissions were kept, which recorded the parish of settlement of the parents, together with the age of the mother. These records are now held at TNA, in series RG 8, and have been digitized. Of the women admitted in September 1754, for example, half had settlements outside the London area, with a wide range of husbands' occupations represented. Those with settlements outside London included:

Elizabeth (33) wife of William Parkhouse, husbandman, of Witheridge, Devonshire.

Mary (31) wife of Thomas Tapley, shoemaker, of Totnes, Devonshire.

Mary (29) wife of William Young, tanner, of Fareham, Hampshire.

Elizabeth (24) wife of George Buck, butcher, of Selwich, Kent.

Sarah (18) wife of Joseph Rogers, perukemaker, of Melcum Regis, Dorset.

Sarah (27) wife of John Werge, clerk, of Hartly Pool [Hartlepool], Durham.

Ann (26) wife of Thomas Fox, soldier, of Newark, Nottinghamshire.

Elizabeth [age omitted] wife of Christopher Liddel, of St Nicholas, Newcastle.

Elizabeth (22) wife of John Brooks, combmaker, of All Hallows, York.

Roads in the early eighteenth century were poor and journeys on land were very slow, but a network of toll roads between major towns, known as *turnpikes*, was established after 1750. Turnpikes reduced journey times and facilitated the expansion of the stagecoach network, which led to the growth of coaching inns, where passengers could obtain refreshments and horses could be changed. Stagecoach travel reached its peak in the last two decades of the Georgian period. Although the improvement of roads enabled goods to be transported more easily, a horse can pull ten times more cargo in a canal boat than in a cart, and many canals were constructed between 1760 and 1830. The expansion of the canal network led to further industrialization in the Midlands and north. The first steam-powered public railway was built in 1825, but railways had relatively little impact on transport before the Victorian era. The transport of goods and people between coastal areas was usually by sea.

Some people who lived in England may at some time have lived in Wales, Scotland or Ireland, and others may have been born there.

Evidence of previous residence elsewhere in the British Isles may be found in a variety of sources discussed in this book. Welsh and English records are virtually identical, many Scottish records are significantly different, and the majority of Irish records for the period no longer survive. Tracing ancestors outside England is beyond the scope of this book, but other books are available that specialize on the sources available for tracing ancestors elsewhere in the British Isles.

Clues to the places of origin of people with uncommon surnames can sometimes be found by establishing the area or areas in which surnames originated. Many English surnames were concentrated in specific areas before the Industrial Revolution, particularly those derived from place names and physical features, such as Coplestone and Haythornthwaite. Further information on surnames in family history can be found in Hey (2000). Many individuals and groups are involved in one-name studies and a considerable amount of information has been collected for some surnames. Many one-name studies are registered with the Guild of One-Name Studies.

IMMIGRATION AND EMIGRATION

Migration did not always involve a one-way journey, and a proportion of migrants eventually returned to their country of origin, in most cases to the places they had left. Clues to overseas residence can sometimes be found in wills, deeds and other records. Information on tracing baptisms, marriages and deaths that occurred overseas can be found in a guide published by the Guildhall Library (1995).

The arrival and presence of immigrants in Georgian England went largely unrecorded, although some records relating to naturalization, denization and the arrival of aliens, mainly after 1800, are held at TNA. As mentioned in Chapter 5, many French Protestants seeking refuge from persecution had settled in England before the Georgian era. Further immigration from France took place after the French Revolution of 1789. These émigrés were from all levels of society and mainly settled in the London area. The union of the thrones of Great Britain and Hanover resulted in a steady trickle of immigrants from German states, mainly merchants and craftsmen who settled in London. Following the occupation of Hanover by French forces in 1803, thousands of soldiers came to England from Germany at the instigation of George III to form the *King's German Legion*, which participated in several campaigns during the Napoleonic War, and took part in the Battle of Waterloo. The infantry base was at Bexhill in Kent and the cavalry base at Weymouth in Dorset, and some men married local women. Although most men returned to Germany after the war, some settled in England. Thousands of black people were living in England by the end of the eighteenth century, most of whom had previously been slaves. Some were employed as domestic servants, and others engaged in a variety of occupations.

Most emigration during the early Georgian period was to North America. Emigration to the thirteen American colonies increased dramatically during the 1760s and early 1770s until the outbreak of the American War of Independence in 1775. Some settlers were Loyalists who did not support independence, many of whom left the United States and settled in Canada where they were subsequently known as United Empire Loyalists, and others returned to Great Britain. Emigration to Canada increased after 1815 as a result of population growth and unemployment in England.

Australia was first settled by Europeans in 1788 when the First Fleet of convicts arrived from England. The migration of free settlers was encouraged after 1815. In the 1830s many poor families in rural areas were given financial assistance to emigrate to Australia and Canada, and records can sometimes be found in Vestry minutes. Very little emigration to New Zealand took place before the 1840s. Some emigration to British colonies occurred as a result of soldiers and sailors who had been stationed there choosing not to return home after completing their service.

Several islands in the Caribbean became British colonies during the seventeenth century, and plantations were established for growing crops such as sugar and tobacco. Although the first plantation workers were white indentured servants, by the beginning of the Georgian era most were black slaves from West Africa. Many people who owned land in the West Indies became very rich through the slave trade. Although the slave trade was abolished in 1807, slavery did not finally come to an end until the 1830s. Some people from England settled in the West Indies, and other members of their families often spent some time there. Many records containing information about settlers are held at TNA. Correspondence between people in England and the Caribbean has often survived in collections of family papers. Titford (2011) describes the sources available for researching British people who settled in the West Indies.

Many employees of the East India Company spent considerable periods of time in India, although few settled there. Most of the relevant records are held at the British Library and many have now been digitized by Findmypast. Further information on researching British people who had a connection with India can be found in Jolly (2012) and biographical sources are listed in Baxter (2004). Information is also available on the website of the Families in British India Society (FIBIS).

Information on the origin of emigrants from England is more likely to be found in the records of the countries in which they settled, but some relevant records are held at TNA. Many records remain unindexed, but some have been digitized by Findmypast as part of the *Early Emigration from Britain 1636-1815* collection. Very few passenger lists are available for the Georgian era, but between 1773 and 1776 the British government required all ports to keep records of emigrants to the American colonies, and these records are held at TNA in series T 47/9-11. The information recorded on each emigrant includes their age, occupation, place of former residence, destination, the ship name, the reason for emigrating and the port and date of embarkation. Over 6,000 emigrants are listed in these records, which are included in the Findmypast Early Emigration collection mentioned above. A transcript of these records has also been published, (Coldham, 1988a), and is available on Ancestry.

Sources held at TNA relating to both immigration and emigration are described in Kershaw (2009).

Chapter 13

RESEARCH METHODS

Successful genealogical research requires not only familiarity with the sources available and some knowledge of the historical context, but also the use of sound research methods. Most family history researchers build up their research skills gradually through carrying out their own research and sometimes by collaborating with more experienced researchers. Many case studies in books and magazines describe the techniques that have been used to overcome brick walls.

The few books on research methods that have been published in recent years have all been written by professional genealogists. Rogers (2008), first published in 1985, takes a problem-solving approach to genealogical research both before and after 1837. Osborn (2012) is an excellent introduction to research methods, and another book by the present author (Wintrip, 2017) focuses on research in the period before 1837 and discusses in more detail many of the topics touched on in this chapter.

SEARCHING FOR BAPTISMS, MARRIAGES AND BURIALS

The traditional procedure for tracing baptisms, marriages and burials involves browsing page by page through original parish registers (or microfilm copies) for an appropriate range of years around the most likely date of the event being sought. This process is repeated parish by parish, in an ever-increasing radius around the parish where the individual or family seems likely to have lived, based on the evidence available, until either a record is found or the search is abandoned as unsuccessful. This procedure requires using maps showing the boundaries of ancient parishes and the existence of any constituent chapelries, together with guides to the availability and whereabouts of parish registers. Bishop's transcripts are searched when necessary to fill in any gaps in coverage.

The initial phase of searching for baptisms, marriages and burials in many areas now involves using online indexes and collections of digitized parish registers available through search services such as Ancestry, Findmypast and FamilySearch. Online searching has the potential to enable records to be identified quickly and easily, but some records that exist in original sources may not be found in online record collections for a variety of reasons. Awareness of the limitations in coverage of particular online record collections, together with an understanding of the principles of traditional parish-by-parish searching, can often enable these records to be found.

It is important to establish the completeness of large online record collections with titles such as 'Lincolnshire Marriages' or 'Wiltshire Baptisms'. Online record collections for some counties include only selected parishes, but this is not always obvious. Some online record collections, usually without associated images, have been produced by family history societies, and are as complete as it is possible to be, based on the extent of surviving records, with any deficiencies in parish registers filled using information from bishop's transcripts.

Online record collections containing digital images of original parish registers usually correspond to the holdings of specific archives, and material is often made available online in batches. Even when a digitization project has been completed, the records for some parishes may not have been included, either because they are still held by churches or because the original registers are in very poor condition. One or two parishes whose registers are held in an archive may have refused permission for them to be digitized. It is therefore necessary to identify any specific parish registers that have not been digitized and to search them individually. This may require using other online search services or visiting archives and libraries where microfilm copies of parish registers or bishop's transcripts are available. As with traditional parish-by-parish searching, ensuring that all parishes and chapelries have been covered requires using parish maps.

Even when original sources are included in online record collections, specific records may not be retrieved, for a variety of reasons, such as the accidental omission of some records, transcription errors, and some unusual name variants not being identified by search systems. When expected records are not retrieved, it is advisable to browse page by page through the original handwritten registers of the most likely parishes. This involves either browsing through the relevant images online or using microfilm copies in archives or libraries. This process may enable some records to be identified that were not retrieved by the search system, and can also provide an explanation for the absence of records in sources where they might have been expected.

Gaps of several weeks or months, during which no events were recorded, are not uncommon in parish registers. When the date of an expected event coincides with such a gap, but all other events relating to a family can be found in the registers of the same parish, and there is no evidence of residence elsewhere, the most likely explanation is that the event took place in the parish but was not recorded. Such gaps are less likely to be found in marriage registers after 1754, as registers had to be signed at the time of the marriage. Surviving bishop's transcripts should always be searched when gaps are found in parish registers, although they may well be found to be equally defective.

FAMILY RECONSTITUTION

The information recorded in the church registers of the Georgian era is often insufficient in itself to enable relationships between individuals of different generations to be established with certainty. Marriage records before 1837 did not record parents' names or the ages of the bride and groom, baptism records did not record the mother's maiden name, and before 1813 not always her Christian name, and burial records before 1813 did not record age. It is more likely to be possible to establish relationships between individuals by investigating whole families than by restricting research only to direct ancestors. In favourable circumstances, it may be possible to incorporate all the individuals in a parish with the same surname into a family tree spanning several generations. This technique is known as family reconstitution, and is described in more detail in Todd (2015). It is important to search burial as well as baptism records and to identify any children who died in infancy or childhood.

Family reconstitution based entirely on records in church registers is more likely to be possible when a family stayed in the same parish, had a relatively uncommon surname, gave children uncommon Christian names, and followed specific naming patterns. It is also more likely to be possible in those parishes in which slightly more detailed baptism and burial records were kept.

It is often entirely coincidental that records for families that include individuals with very similar names and ages can be found in two different areas, which seem to fit together, but such records do sometimes relate to only one family. It may be possible to establish that they were, even without any specific evidence for migration, if there is such a strong correlation between baptism, marriage and burial records in the area of origin and those in the destination area that no other explanation could be possible.

Establishing the relationship of witnesses to the bride and groom for those marriages that took place after 1754 can sometimes be helpful in family reconstitution. Although the identity of witnesses was not recorded, relatives can often be identified. When people signed their names rather than making their marks it may be possible to compare their signatures with those in other marriage records and other types of record in which signatures can be found, such as original wills, marriage licence documents and deeds.

In less favourable circumstances, it may not be possible to establish relationships between individuals with the same surname, and who are likely to have been closely related, based solely on records in parish registers. Because of the minimal information recorded in marriage registers, it can be particularly difficult to establish the correct baptism records for people whose marriages have been identified, and in some cases no likely baptism record can be found.

A common error made by researchers moving back into the Georgian era is to assume that a baptism record and a marriage record for two people with the same name and living in the same area that seem to fit together must relate to the same person because they were the only records they could find, but without seeking further evidence or considering alternative explanations. Researchers who are more interested in 'getting back further' than carrying out sound research are more likely to identify the wrong ancestors.

Family reconstitution may enable records to be linked together without ambiguity in a sparsely-populated rural area, but the probability that two records for the same name relate to the same person decreases as the size and mobility of the population increases. In an area with a large or transient population there is a significant probability that a person who had been born in the area might have left and been 'replaced' by another person of similar age with the same name moving into the area who subsequently married there. However, the existence of only one baptism and marriage record gives the illusion of only one person, which can result in researchers tracing several previous generations of people who were not actually their ancestors.

Some children were not baptized in infancy, some may have been baptized but the baptism was not recorded, and some baptism registers have not survived, particularly those for Nonconformist congregations. It is therefore inevitable that baptism records will not be found for a proportion of people born during the Georgian era. When church records cannot be found, or provide insufficient information, evidence of the relationship between individuals may be available in other types of source, discussed in this book, and new information may be found in the future as more sources become searchable by name.

SEARCH TOOLS

The chances of finding relevant information can be increased by becoming familiar with the full range of search tools that are available for the area concerned. These can be grouped into several categories:

- Large online search services, either free or requiring a subscription, such as FamilySearch, FreeReg, Findmypast, Ancestry and The Genealogist.
- Specialized online search services focusing on specific themes or geographical areas, either requiring payment or available only to members of certain organizations, such as family history societies. One example of a fee-based service focusing on a specific area is Durham Records Online.
- Indexes and searchable transcripts, in printed, microfiche and CD format, and increasingly as files in electronic format that can be downloaded, available for purchase from individuals and family history societies, and/or through specialist online vendors such as GENfair and Parish Chest.
- Bespoke fee-based search services, of records in unique 'private' indexes and databases, offered by individuals and family history societies.
- Miscellaneous published, typescript, manuscript and card indexes, available in selected libraries and archives, and sometimes in only one.
- Archive catalogues (discussed in the following section).

Understanding and using the advanced search features of online search tools can often enable records to be identified that are not retrieved when using the basic search system. It can therefore be worthwhile studying database guides and help pages. Searching for name variants is a major challenge, and online search services offer various different methods for retrieving them, sometimes offering a choice between 'exact match', 'close variants' and 'wide variants'. However, not all name variants are necessarily retrieved by such systems, so it is advisable to search separately for any known variants that do not appear to have been retrieved automatically.

Finding information in sources other than church registers is often the key to making further progress in the Georgian era, but they are not all searchable online. Search tools for some sources are only available in printed format, or as typescript, manuscript or card indexes available only in specific archives or libraries. It may be feasible to browse through sources that have not been indexed at all if they are not too large, or a clue can be found indicating the specific section in which a record is likely to be found.

USING ARCHIVES

Unlike libraries, in which readers can browse the shelves to see what is available, archives are like retail catalogue showrooms, in which customers must use catalogues to identify the items they require. Catalogues are the key to finding information in archives, but many archives have more than one, and most have a range of other finding aids.

Before computerized catalogues became available, most archive services listed their holdings in typescript paper catalogues set out in the form of hierarchical inventories, usually with the provision of alphabetical card indexes for names and places. In the early twenty-first century, when few archives had their own online catalogues, selected paper catalogues of many English and Welsh archives were converted into electronic format during the *Access to Archives* (A2A) project. The records are now included in TNA's *Discovery* catalogue, which also lists TNA's own holdings.

Most archives have introduced their own online catalogues in recent years, and have converted some or all of their existing paper catalogues into electronic format. There are varying degrees of overlap between Discovery and the dedicated online catalogues now available for the majority of archives, but Discovery still provides the only online search facility for some archives. The *Archives Hub* is a union catalogue of archives in academic institutions, which may enable some resources in unexpected archives to be identified, such as collections of family papers.

The holdings of many archives are still only partially searchable online, and a small number do not yet provide any online searching facility. Identifying relevant material may therefore require using a range of catalogues and other finding aids, some of which may only be accessible at archive premises. Paper catalogues are still available in many archives, even those with online catalogues, as they permit more rapid browsing of the contents of whole record collections. Further details of the range of search tools available for specific archives can usually be found on their websites, but it can often be beneficial to contact archives in advance of a visit to confirm what resources and finding aids are available. Enquiries about holdings, as opposed to actual research in them, are usually answered free of charge. Some archive services provide catalogue training sessions and others offer courses on using archives in genealogical research.

There can be considerable variation in the level of detail to which record collections have been listed, even within a single archive. Each physically-separate item in some record collections may have been listed, but only bundles or boxes in others. Identifying relevant items by searching for specific names in archive catalogues is therefore dependent on the level of detail to which record collections have been listed.

A large number of major genealogical sources held by archives, such as parish registers and wills, have been filmed by the LDS, and most of the microfilms that were made in the past are in the process of being digitized. Because of licensing restrictions, some digital images are only viewable on computers physically located in LDS family history centres. There are about fifty family history centres in England, so people living some distance away from archives where original sources are held may be able to carry out some research locally that would otherwise require travelling to the areas concerned. The London FamilySearch Centre is the largest family history centre in England, but most others are small, with limited opening hours, and usually require appointments to be made.

The library at the Society of Genealogists in London is the largest genealogical library in England. It holds a large collection of microfilm copies of original sources, as well as transcripts, indexes and a range of other genealogical resources. As an official LDS Affiliate Library, it also provides access to the digitized resources that are only viewable at LDS family history centres.

Paying to have research carried out may be a cost-effective option when personal research would otherwise involve expenditure on travel and accommodation. Some archive services offer in-house research services, and many independent researchers carry out paid research in archives. The knowledge and experience of independent researchers is very variable, so without a specific recommendation it is advisable to choose a researcher with an advanced qualification in genealogy or who is a Member of the Association of Genealogists and Researchers in Archives (AGRA). AGRA is the only organization for professional genealogists in England and Wales to require proof of competence as a condition of membership. As well as carrying out research in archives, many professional genealogists offer other services, such as transcribing old documents.

Appendix 1

TIMELINE

This is not a chronology of major historical events, but a list of dates of particular relevance to people researching their ancestry in Georgian England.

1714   Accession of George I.

1727   Death of George I and accession of his son George II.

1745–6   Jacobite Rebellion.

1752   Change from the Julian to the Gregorian Calendar.

1754   Hardwicke's Marriage Act comes into effect.

1756   Outbreak of the Seven Years War.

1757   Establishment of the 'New Militia'.

1760   Death of George II and accession of his grandson George III.

1763   End of the Seven Years War.

1775   Outbreak of the American War of Independence.

1778   Outbreak of war with France. Catholic Relief Act removes many restrictions on Roman Catholics.

1780   Anti-Catholic Gordon Riots in London.

1782   Gilbert's Act permits groups of parishes to set up poorhouses.

1783   End of the American War of Independence and war with France.
Stamp Duty Act imposes a duty on entries in parish registers.

1787   First fleet of convicts sails for Australia.

1789   Outbreak of the French Revolution.

1791   Catholic Relief Act enables chapels to be registered as places of worship.

1793   Outbreak of the French Revolutionary War.

1794   Repeal of the Stamp Duty Act.

1795   Introduction of the Speenhamland system of poor relief.

1798   Irish Rebellion.

1801   Acts of Union between Great Britain and Ireland come into effect.

1802   Peace of Amiens ends the French Revolutionary War (March).

1803   Outbreak of the Napoleonic War (May).

1805   Battle of Trafalgar.

1811   George, Prince of Wales (later George IV), becomes Prince Regent.

1811–12 Luddite disturbances.

1812   Outbreak of the War of 1812 with the United States.

1813   George Rose's Act comes into effect.

1814   Abdication of Napoleon and temporary cessation of hostilities with France.

1815   End of the war with the United States. 'Hundred Days' (March–June) culminating in the Battle of Waterloo.

1819   Sturges Bourne Act permits parishes to set up Select Vestries with responsibility for poor relief. Peterloo Massacre in Manchester.

1820   Death of George III and accession of his son George IV.

1829   Catholic Emancipation Act.

1830   Death of George IV and accession of his brother William IV. Swing riots.

1831   Reform Bill riots.

1832   Great Reform Act.

1834   Transportation of the Tolpuddle Martyrs. Poor Law Amendment Act.

1835   Municipal Corporations Act.

1837   Death of William IV and accession of his niece Victoria.

Appendix 2

GLOSSARY

This is a selected list of terms commonly found in records of the Georgian era that may be unfamiliar to people who have not previously carried out research in this period. Some words are included that are still in use today, but whose meaning has changed over time. Archaic occupations are not included.

A.B. (after a name)	Artium Baccalaureus = Bachelor of Arts (BA), often denoting an Anglican clergyman.
Act Book	A volume containing summaries of the activities of an ecclesiastical jurisdiction or church court.
A.M. (after a name)	Artium Magister = Master of Arts (MA), often denoting an Anglican clergyman.
archdeaconry	A subdivision of a diocese consisting of several deaneries.
archdiocese	An area under the authority of an archbishop, consisting of a number of dioceses, also known as an archbishopric or province.
Assize courts	Criminal courts held locally that dealt with more serious cases, presided over by judges from London, and usually held twice each year.
attorney	A lawyer in the courts of common law.
bona notabilia	An estate valued at (usually) £5 or more (literally 'considerable goods').

bond	A legal agreement requiring one or more individuals to pay a penal sum if they fail to fulfil certain conditions.
burgess	A freeman of a borough; an MP representing a borough.
cause	A case before an church court.
chapel of ease	A subsidiary church building in a large parish.
chapelry	A church serving a specific area within a larger parish, functioning in most respects as a separate parish.
Chelsea Pensioner	A former soldier receiving a pension from the Royal Hospital, Chelsea, either resident (an in-pensioner) or non-resident (an out-pensioner).
clandestine marriage	A marriage not preceded by the calling of banns or the obtaining of a marriage licence.
clerk (in holy orders)	An Anglican clergyman.
Clerk of the Peace	A man, usually a lawyer, responsible for Quarter Sessions records.
consistory court	A diocesan court with jurisdiction over probate and other matters.
Constable	A parish officer with a variety of duties relating to law and order, appointed annually, and usually unpaid.
copyhold	A type of landholding in a manor.
cornet	The lowest rank of commissioned officer in cavalry regiments, equivalent to a second lieutenant.
Court Baron	A manorial court concerned with the transfer of land.
Court Leet	A manorial court concerned with disciplinary matters and the punishment of minor offences.
cousin	A relation by blood or marriage.

daughter-in-law	The wife of a son or a step-daughter.
dean	The senior clergyman of a cathedral or rural deanery.
dean and chapter	The governing body of a cathedral.
deanery	A group of adjacent parishes within a diocese.
diocese	An area under the authority of a bishop, consisting of a number of archdeaconries.
dissenter	A Protestant Nonconformist.
enclosure	Reorganization of land, including open fields in multiple ownership, commons and wastes, into discrete units owned by individuals, often by Act of Parliament.
ensign	The lowest rank of commissioned officer in infantry regiments, equivalent to a second lieutenant.
Esquire (after a name)	A landowner of higher status than a gentleman; a Lord of the Manor; a man of high occupational status such as a barrister.
examinant	A person being examined under oath.
extra-parochial place	An area not part of any parish and whose residents did not pay church rates, poor rates or tithes.
farthing	A quarter of a penny.
fine	An initial sum paid by a new copyhold tenant.
folio	A sheet of paper or parchment numbered only on the front side.
freeman	A man having certain rights and privileges in a city or borough.
friends	Anyone, including family members, having a close relationship with a person and not acting in any official capacity.

gentleman	A landowner of higher status than a yeoman but below an Esquire; a man with a private income.
Greenwich Pensioner	A former Royal Navy sailor or Royal Marine receiving a pension from Greenwich Hospital, either resident (an in-pensioner) or non-resident (an out-pensioner).
guinea	One pound one shilling.
hundred	A subdivision of a county.
husbandman	A tenant farmer.
indenture	A contract between two or more parties written on a sheet of parchment with an indentured (wavy) edge, produced by cutting a single sheet on which the contract had been written two or more times, with one piece given to each party.
infant	In a legal sense, a person under the age of 21.
instant	The present month.
invalid	A soldier unfit for active service but capable of garrison duty.
Justice of the Peace	A magistrate, usually one of the gentry or an Anglican clergyman.
Knight of the Shire	One of the two MPs representing a county in Parliament.
Lady Day	25 March.
lease and release	A method of transferring the ownership of land, consisting of two documents dated on consecutive days.
liberty	An area within the boundaries of a county but not under its jurisdiction.
livery company	A trade association in the City of London.
lying in	Childbirth and ensuing bed-rest.
manor	A landed estate with feudal origins.

messuage	A dwelling house and its outbuildings.
Michaelmas	29 September.
Midsummer Day	24 June.
militia	County-based military units serving part-time during peacetime and embodied for home defence during wartime.
Mr (Master, Mister)	In the earlier Georgian era a title only applicable to men of higher social status, usually those having authority over others.
Mrs (Mistress)	In the earlier Georgian era a title only applicable to women of higher social status, and not indicative of marital status.
natural child	The child of unmarried parents, but often acknowledged by the father and sometimes taking his surname.
North Britain	Scotland.
out-pensioner	A non-resident pensioner of the Royal Hospital, Chelsea or Greenwich Hospital.
Parish Clerk	A layman with a variety of paid responsibilities within a parish.
parochial chapelry	A church serving a specific area within a larger parish, functioning in most respects as a separate parish.
peculiar	A parish within the boundaries of a diocese but not under the jurisdiction of its bishop.
penny	The twelfth part of a shilling.
pensioner	A former soldier or sailor receiving a pension; an elderly pauper receiving regular parish relief; a student at the University of Cambridge paying for his board and lodging.
Petty Sessions	Local courts presided over by two or more Justices of the Peace, dealing with petty crimes and Poor Law matters.

prerogative court	A probate court of the Archdiocese of Canterbury or York.
private baptism	A baptism not performed in a church building.
proctor	A lawyer in a church court.
province	An area under the authority of an archbishop, consisting of a number of dioceses, also known as an archdiocese or archbishopric.
proximo	The next month.
quarter days	Lady Day, Midsummer Day, Michaelmas and Christmas Day.
Quarter Sessions	Quarterly courts held in counties and some cities and boroughs presided over by Justices of the Peace, dealing with criminal offences, Poor Law disputes, and administrative matters.
real property	Land and any associated buildings, crops and other immovable features resulting from human activity.
recognizance	A bond requiring a person or persons to fulfil certain conditions.
relict	A widow.
rural deanery	A group of adjacent parishes.
shilling	The twentieth part of a pound, consisting of twelve pence.
solicitor	A lawyer in the courts of equity.
son-in-law	The husband of a daughter or a step-son.
surrogate	An ecclesiastical lawyer or clergyman with authority to perform certain duties, such as proving wills or issuing marriage licences.
tail male	Restriction of inheritance to male heirs.
tithes	Payments made by parishioners for the support of clergy, originally paid in kind, but later in money.

tithing	Originally a subdivision of a manor, but by the Georgian era generally a subdivision of a parish.
Tithingman	Originally the head of a manorial tithing, with responsibility for keeping the peace, but by the Georgian era generally the Constable of a parish or a subdivision of a parish.
township	A subdivision of a parish with civil responsibilities, such as poor relief.
turnpike	A toll road.
ultimo	The previous month.
Vestry	The 'council' of a parish, consisting of the incumbent and principal inhabitants, responsible for both ecclesiastical and civil matters, including the appointment of parish officers.
Volunteers	Local volunteer infantry liable to be called up in the event of an invasion.
wapentake	A subdivision in some counties (e.g. Yorkshire and Lincolnshire), similar to a hundred.
ward	A subdivision in the counties of Cumberland, Westmorland, Northumberland and Durham.
yeoman	A farmer owning his own land.
Yeomanry	Local volunteer cavalry liable to be called up in the event of an invasion, sometimes used to deal with social unrest in the absence of a police force.

BIBLIOGRAPHY

Dates of publication and availability in print do not necessarily reflect the continuing usefulness of specialist genealogy books. Titles that are now out of print can be found in major libraries, and second-hand copies can usually be purchased through online booksellers.

Adolph, A. (2013) *Tracing Your Aristocratic Ancestors.* Barnsley: Pen & Sword.

Alcock, N. (2017) *Tracing History Through Title Deeds.* Barnsley: Pen & Sword.

Aldous, V.E. (1999) *My Ancestors Were Freemen of the City of London.* London: Society of Genealogists.

Atkins, P.J. (1990) *The Directories of London 1677-1977.* London: Mansell Publishing.

Bailey, P.A. (2006) *Researching Ancestors in the East India Company Armies.* [s.l.]: Families in British India Society.

Barrow, G.B. (1977) *The Genealogist's Guide: An Index to Printed British Pedigrees and Family Histories, 1950-1975.* London: Research Publishing Co.

Baxter, I.A. (2004) *Baxter's Guide: Biographical Sources in the India Office Records.* 3rd ed. [s.l.]: Families in British India Society.

Bevan, A. (2006) *Tracing Your Ancestors in the National Archives.* Kew: The National Archives.

Bourne, S. and Chicken, A.H. (1994) *Records of the Medical Professions: A Practical Guide for the Family Historian.* [Self-published].

Breed, G.R. (2002) *My Ancestors Were Baptists.* 4th ed. London: Society of Genealogists.

Bromley, J. and Bromley, D. (2011) *Wellington's Men Remembered*. Vols 1–2. Barnsley: Pen & Sword.

Brooks, B. and Herber, M. (2006) *My Ancestor Was a Lawyer*. London: Society of Genealogists.

Brooks, R. and Little, M. (2008) *Tracing Your Royal Marine Ancestors*. Barnsley: Pen & Sword.

Burlison, R. (2009) *Tracing Your Pauper Ancestors*. Barnsley: Pen & Sword.

Chapman, C.R. (1997) *Sin, Sex and Probate: Ecclesiastical Courts, Officials and Records.* 2nd ed. Dursley: Lochin Publishing.

Chapman, C.R. (2002) *Pre-1841 Censuses and Population Listings in the British Isles.* 5th ed. reprinted with minor additions. Dursley: Lochin Publishing.

Chater, K. (2012) *Tracing Your Huguenot Ancestors*. Barnsley: Pen & Sword.

Clifford, D.J.H. (1997) *My Ancestors Were Congregationalists in England and Wales.* 2nd ed. London: Society of Genealogists.

Coldham, P.W. (1988a) *Emigrants from England to the American Colonies, 1773-1776.* Baltimore: Genealogical Publishing Company.

Coldham, P.W. (1988b) *The Complete Book of Emigrants in Bondage, 1614-1775.* Baltimore: Genealogical Publishing Company.

Coldham, P.W. (2002) *More Emigrants in Bondage, 1614-1775.* Baltimore: Genealogical Publishing Company.

Currer-Briggs, N. and Gambier, R. (1985) *Huguenot Ancestry*. Chichester: Phillimore.

Divall, K. (2008) *My Ancestor Was a Royal Marine*. London: Society of Genealogists.

Erickson, A.L. (2012) *Mistresses and Marriage: Or, a Short History of the Mrs.* (Working Papers from Department of Economic and Social History at the University of Cambridge, No 8.) Available from: http://EconPapers.repec.org/RePEc:cmh:wpaper:06

Forrest, M. (2011) *Dorset Manorial Documents*. Dorchester: Dorset Record Society.

Fowler, S. (2011) *Tracing Your Naval Ancestors*. Barnsley: Pen & Sword.

Fowler, S. (2017) *Tracing Your Army Ancestors*. 3rd ed. Barnsley: Pen & Sword.

Gandy, M. (1993) *Catholic Missions and Registers 1700-1880.* (6 volumes) London: M. Gandy.

Gibson, J. (2001) *Bishops' Transcripts and Marriage Licences, Bonds and Allegations.* 5th ed. Bury: Federation of Family History Societies.

Gibson, J. et al. (2004) *Land and Window Tax Assessments, 1690-1950.* Updated 2nd ed. Bury: Federation of Family History Societies.

Gibson, J. (2007) *Quarter Sessions Records for Family Historians.* 5th ed. Bury: The Family History Partnership.

Gibson, J. and Rogers, C. (2008) *Poll Books 1696-1872: A Directory of Holdings in Great Britain.* 4th ed. Bury: The Family History Partnership.

Gibson, J. and Medlycott, M. (2013) *Militia Lists and Musters.* 5th ed. Bury: The Family History Partnership.

Gibson, J. and Raymond, S. (2016) *Probate Jurisdictions: Where to Look for Wills.* 6th ed. Bury: The Family History Partnership.

Grannum, K. and Taylor, N. (2009) *Wills and Probate Records.* Kew: The National Archives.

Guildhall Library (1995) *The British Overseas: A Guide to Records of their Births, Baptisms, Marriages, Deaths and Burials, Available in the United Kingdom.* 3rd ed. London: Guildhall Library.

Hawkings, D.T. (2003) *Fire Insurance Records for Family and Local Historians.* London: Francis Boutle.

Hawkings, D.T. (2009) *Criminal Ancestors: A Guide to Historical Criminal Records in England and Wales.* Stroud: History Press.

Hawkings, D.T. (2011) *Pauper Ancestors: A Guide to the Records Created by the Poor Laws in England and Wales.* Stroud: History Press.

Hawkings, D.T. (2012) *Bound for Australia: A Guide to the Records of Transported Convicts and Early Settlers.* Stroud: History Press.

Hey, D. (2000) *Family Names and Family History.* London: Hambledon and London.

Higgs, M. (2011) *Tracing Your Medical Ancestors.* Barnsley: Pen & Sword.

Hindle, P. (1998) *Maps for Historians.* Chichester: Phillimore.

Holborn, G. (1999) *Sources of Biographical Information on Past Lawyers.* Warwick: British and Irish Association of Law Librarians.

Hollowell, S. (2000) *Enclosure Records for Historians*. Chichester: Phillimore.

Humphery-Smith, C.R. (2003) *The Phillimore Atlas and Index of Parish Registers*. 3rd ed. Chichester: Phillimore.

Jolly, E. (2012) *Tracing Your British Indian Ancestors*. Barnsley: Pen & Sword.

Kain, R.J.P. and Prince, H.C. (2000) *Tithe Surveys for Historians*. Chichester: Phillimore.

Kershaw, R. (2009) *Migration Records: A Guide for Family Historians*. Kew: The National Archives.

Leary, W. (2005) *My Ancestors Were Methodists*. 4th ed. London: Society of Genealogists.

Lewis, P. (2012) *My Ancestor Was a Freemason*. 4th ed. London: Society of Genealogists.

Marshall, G.W. (1903) *The Genealogist's Guide*. Guildford: Billing.

Marshall, H. (2004) *Palaeography for Local and Family Historians*. 2nd ed. Chichester: Phillimore.

Masters, C. (2009) *Essential Maps for Family Historians*. Newbury: Countryside Books.

Milligan, E.H. and Thomas, M.J. (1999) *My Ancestors Were Quakers*. 2nd ed. London: Society of Genealogists.

Moore, S.T. (2017) *Tracing Your Ancestors Through the Equity Courts*. Barnsley: Pen & Sword.

Mullett, M. (1991) *Sources for the History of English Nonconformity 1660-1830*. [London]: British Records Association.

Norton, J.E. (1984) *Guide to the National and Provincial Directories of England and Wales, Excluding London, Published Before 1856*. London: Offices of the Royal Historical Society.

Oates, J. (2017) *Tracing Villains and their Victims*. Barnsley: Pen & Sword.

Oates, P. (2003) *My Ancestors Were Inghamites*. London: Society of Genealogists.

Osborn, H. (2012) *Genealogy: Essential Research Methods*. London: Robert Hale.

Paley, R. (2004) *My Ancestor Was a Bastard*. London: Society of Genealogists.

Pappalardo, B. (2001) *Royal Navy Lieutenants' Passing Certificates (1691-1902)*. London: List & Index Society.

Pappalardo, B. (2003) *Tracing Your Naval Ancestors*. Kew: Public Record Office.

Probert, R. (2016) *Marriage Law for Genealogists.* 2nd ed. Kenilworth: Takeaway.

Ratcliffe, R. (2014) *Methodist Records for Family Historians*. Bury: The Family History Partnership.

Raymond, S.A. (2010) *My Ancestor Was an Apprentice*. London: Society of Genealogists.

Raymond, S.A. (2012a) *My Ancestor Was a Gentleman*. London: Society of Genealogists.

Raymond, S.A. (2012b) *The Wills of Our Ancestors*. Barnsley: Pen & Sword.

Raymond, S.A. (2015) *Tracing Your Ancestors' Parish Records*. Barnsley: Pen & Sword.

Raymond, S.A. (2016) *Tracing Your Ancestors in County Records*. Barnsley: Pen & Sword.

Raymond, S.A. (2017a) *Tracing Your Nonconformist Ancestors*. Barnsley: Pen & Sword.

Raymond, S.A. (2017b) *Tracing Your Church of England Ancestors*. Barnsley: Pen & Sword.

Raymond, S.A. (forthcoming) *Tracing Your Roman Catholic Ancestors*. Barnsley: Pen & Sword.

Rodger, N.A.M. (1988) *Naval Records for Genealogists*. Kew: PRO Publications.

Rogers, C.D. (2008) *The Family Tree Detective*. 4th ed. Manchester: Manchester University Press.

Ruston, A.R. (2001) *My Ancestors Were English Presbyterians or Unitarians*. 2nd ed. London: Society of Genealogists.

Scott, M. (1997) *Prerogative Court of Canterbury Wills and Other Probate Records*. Kew: PRO Publications.

Smith, K. et al. (1998) *Records of Merchant Shipping and Seamen*. Kew: PRO Publications.

Spencer, W. (1997) *Records of the Militia and Volunteer Forces 1757-1945*. Kew: PRO Publications.

Spencer, W. (2008) *Army Records: A Guide for Family Historians*. Kew: The National Archives.

Steel, D.J. (1973) *Sources for Nonconformist Genealogy and Family History* (National Index of Parish Registers Volume 2). London: Phillimore.

Steel, D.J. (1976) *General Sources of Births, Marriages and Deaths Before 1837* (National Index of Parish Registers Volume 1). London: Phillimore.

Steel, D.J. and Samuel, E.R. (1974) *Sources for Roman Catholic and Jewish Genealogy and Family History* (National Index of Parish Registers Volume 3). London: Phillimore.

Tarver, A. (1995) *Church Court Records: An Introduction for Family and Local Historians*. Chichester: Phillimore.

Tate, W.E. (1969) *The Parish Chest: A Study of the Records of Parochial Administration in England*. 3rd ed. Cambridge: Cambridge University Press.

Titford, J. (2011) *My Ancestor Settled in the British West Indies*. London: Society of Genealogists.

Todd, A. (2015) *Family History Nuts and Bolts: Problem-Solving Through Family Reconstitution Techniques*. 3rd ed. Ramsbottom: Andrew Todd.

Towey, P. (2006) *My Ancestor Was an Anglican Clergyman*. London: Society of Genealogists.

Wade, S. (2009) *Tracing Your Criminal Ancestors*. Barnsley: Pen & Sword.

Wade, S. (2010) *Tracing Your Legal Ancestors*. Barnsley: Pen & Sword.

Waller, I.H. (2014) *My Ancestor Was in the Royal Navy*. London: Society of Genealogists.

Wallis, P.J. and Wallis, R.V. (1988) *Eighteenth Century Medics: Subscriptions, Licences, Apprenticeships*. Newcastle upon Tyne: Project for Historical Bibliography.

Watts, C.T. and Watts, M.J. (2002) *My Ancestor Was a Merchant Seaman*. 2nd ed. London: Society of Genealogists.

Watts, M.J. and Watts, C.T. (2009) *My Ancestor Was in the British Army*. 2nd ed. London: Society of Genealogists.

Webb, C. (1989) *Dates and Calendars for the Genealogist*. London: Society of Genealogists.

Westcott, B. (2014) *Making Sense of Latin Documents for Family and Local Historians*. Bury: The Family History Partnership.

Whitmore, J.B. (1953) *A Genealogical Guide*. London: Walford.

Wintrip, J. (2017) *Tracing Your Pre-Victorian Ancestors: A Guide to Research Methods for Family Historians*. Barnsley: Pen & Sword.

Wormleighton, T. (2012) *Title Deeds for Family Historians*. Bury: The Family History Partnership.

Worrall, E.S. (1980) *Returns of Papists, 1767. Volume 1: Diocese of Chester*. London: Catholic Record Society.

Worrall, E.S. (1989) *Returns of Papists, 1767. Volume 2: Dioceses of England and Wales, except Chester*. London: Catholic Record Society.

INDEX